GOD THE ALL-IMAGINER

BOOKS OF ORIGINAL AND TRANSLATED VERSE
BY MARTIN BIDNEY

Series: East-West Bridge Builders

Volume I: *East-West Poetry:*
A Western Poet Responds to Islamic Tradition in Sonnets,
Hymns, and Songs
State University of New York Press

Volume II: J. W. von Goethe, *East-West Divan:*
The Poems, with "Notes and Essays":
Goethe's Intercultural Dialogues
(translation from the German with
original verse commentaries)
State University of New York Press

Volume III: *Poems of Wine and Tavern Romance:*
A Dialogue with the Persian Poet Hafiz
(translated from von Hammer's German versions,
with original verse commentaries)
State University of New York Press

Volume IV: *A Unifying Light:*
Lyrical Responses to the Qur'an
Dialogic Poetry Press

Volume V: *The Boundless and the Beating Heart*
Friedrich Rückert's *The Wisdom of the Brahman*
Books 1–4
Dialogic Poetry Press

Volume VI: *God the All-Imaginer:*
Wisdom of Sufi Master Ibn Arabi in 99 Modern Sonnets
(with new translations of his Three Mystic Odes,
27 full-page calligraphies by Shahid Alam)
Dialogic Poetry Press

GOD THE ALL-IMAGINER

∼

Wisdom of Sufi Master Ibn Arabi in 99 Modern Sonnets

with new translations of his Three Mystic Odes

by **MARTIN BIDNEY**

∼

27 full-page calligraphies
by SHAHID ALAM

Dialogic
Poetry
Press

Other Books by Martin Bidney

*Shakespair: Sonnet Replies to the 154 Sonnets
of William Shakespeare*
Dialogic Poetry Press

Alexander Pushkin, *Like a Fine Rug of Erivan: West-East Poems*
(trilingual with audio, co-translated from Russian and
co-edited with Bidney's Introduction)
Mommsen Foundation / Global Scholarly Publications

Saul Tchernikhovsky, *Lyrical Tales and Poems of Jewish Life*
(translated from the Russian versions of Vladislav Khodasevich)
Keshet Press

A Poetic Dialogue with Adam Mickiewicz: The "Crimean Sonnets"
(translated from the Polish, with Sonnet Preface,
Sonnet Replies, and Notes)
Bernstein-Verlag Bonn

Enrico Corsi and Francesca Gambino, *Divine Adventure:
The Fantastic Travels of Dante*
(English verse rendition of the prose translation
by Maria Vera Properzi-Altschuler)
Idea Publications

[For e-books of verse and works of criticism see martinbidney.com]

Copyright © 2016 by Martin Bidney
Dialogic Poetry Press
Vestal, New York

All Rights Reserved

ISBN 13: 978-1533344779
ISBN 10: 1533344779

Printed in the United States of America

Available from Amazon at
http://www.amazon.com/dp/1533344779

The translator dedicates these lyrics
to his dear friend and mentor in Sufi wisdom,
the artist and calligrapher

Shahid Alam

Contents

Introduction: God the All-Imaginer   xiii
  (1) Situating Ibn Arabi in Context   xiii
  (2) A Method of Epiphany Analysis   xviii
  (3) Elemental Impulse: The Lover's Longing Sigh
      of Sadness   xx
  (4) Motion Pattern: Nano-Second Alterations   xxxiv
  (5) Semi-Abstract Images: Line, Point and Plane   xxxvii
  (6) My Dramatic Monologue Sonnet Form   xliii
  (7) Ibn Arabi's Three Mystic Odes   xlvi
  (8) The Beauty of Love in Calligraphy   li

Parables   1
  (1) Ibn Arabi Speaks   3
  (2) Ibn Arabi Tells of Angels   4
  (3) Ibn Arabi Tells of the Face   5
  (4) Ibn Arabi Tells of Families   6
  (5) Ibn Arabi Tells of Light and Wind   7
  (6) Ibn Arabi Tells of the Horn   8
  (7) Ibn Arabi Tells of Breath   9
  (8) Ibn Arabi Tells of Tasting   10
  (9) Ibn Arabi Tells of the Names of Adam   11
  (10) Ibn Arabi Tells of Throwing   12
  (11) Ibn Arabi Tells of Shared Being   13
  (12) Ibn Arabi Tells of Movement   14
  (13) Ibn Arabi Tells of Beliefs   15
  (14) Ibn Arabi Tells of the Sun and Moon   16
  (15) Ibn Arabi Tells of the Chameleon   17

(16) Ibn Arabi Tells of the Unique	18
(17) Ibn Arabi Tells of Milk	19
(18) Ibn Arabi Tells of a Cave	20
(19) Ibn Arabi Tells of Iron and Ruby	21
(20) Ibn Arabi Tells of Boredom	22
(21) Ibn Arabi Tells of Modesty	23
(22) Ibn Arabi Tells of the Root	24
(23) Ibn Arabi Tells of the Waystations	25
(24) Ibn Arabi Tells of the Cup	26
(25) Ibn Arabi Tells of the Knot	27
(26) Ibn Arabi Tells of Imagination	28
(27) Ibn Arabi Tells of the Heart	29
(28) Ibn Arabi Tells of Faith	30
(29) Ibn Arabi Tells of Poverty	31
(30) Ibn Arabi Tells of the Straight Path	32
(31) Ibn Arabi Tells of Time	33
(32) Ibn Arabi Tells of Prayer	34
(33) Ibn Arabi Tells of Three Talismans	35
(34) Ibn Arabi Tells of Master and Sons	36
(35) Ibn Arabi Tells of Courtesy	37
(36) Ibn Arabi Tells of Struggle	38
(37) Ibn Arabi Tells of the Polished Surface	39
(38) Ibn Arabi Tells of the King's Command	40
(39) Ibn Arabi Tells of the Form in the Mirror	41
(40) Ibn Arabi Tells of the Two Eyes	42
(41) Ibn Arabi Tells of Recompense	43
(42) Ibn Arabi Tells of the Lover's Names	44
(43) Ibn Arabi Tells of Treasuries	45
(44) Ibn Arabi Tells of Darkness Visible	46
(45) Ibn Arabi Tells of the Council	47
(46) Ibn Arabi Tells of the Divine Marriage	48
(47) Ibn Arabi Tells of the Lines of Light	49
(48) Ibn Arabi Tells of Even and Odd	50
(49) Ibn Arabi Tells of the Singular Manifold	51
(50) Ibn Arabi Tells of the Two Bows' Length	52
(51) Ibn Arabi Tells of Patience	53

Bezels, or Gem Settings *with Calligraphies*	**55**
of the Prophets' Names by Shahid Alam	
(52) Ibn Arabi Tells of Adam	56
Figure 1. Adam	*57*
(53) Ibn Arabi Tells of Seth	58
Figure 2. Seth	*59*
(54) Ibn Arabi Tells of Noah	60
Figure 3. Noah	*61*
(55) Ibn Arabi Tells of Idris (Enoch)	62
Figure 4. Idris	*63*
(56) Ibn Arabi Tells of Abraham	64
Figure 5. Abraham	*65*
(57) Ibn Arabi Tells of Isaac	66
Figure 6. Isaac	*67*
(58) Ibn Arabi Tells of Ishmael	68
Figure 7. Ishmael	*69*
(59) Ibn Arabi Tells of Jacob	70
Figure 8. Jacob	*71*
(60) Ibn Arabi Tells of Joseph	72
Figure 9. Joseph	*73*
(61) Ibn Arabi Tells of Hūd	74
Figure 10. Hūd	*75*
(62) Ibn Arabi Tells of Ṣāliḥ	76
Figure 11. Ṣāliḥ	*77*
(63) Ibn Arabi Tells of Shuʻaib	78
Figure 12. Shuʻaib	*79*
(64) Ibn Arabi Tells of Lot	80
Figure 13. Lot	*81*
(65) Ibn Arabi Tells of ʻUzair (Ezra)	82
Figure 14. ʻUzair	*83*
(66) Ibn Arabi Tells of Jesus	84
Figure 15. Jesus	*85*
(67) Ibn Arabi Tells of Solomon	86
Figure 16. Solomon	*87*
(68) Ibn Arabi Tells of David	88
Figure 17. David	*89*

(69) Ibn Arabi Tells of Jonah — 90
Figure 18. Jonah — *91*
(70) Ibn Arabi Tells of Job — 92
Figure 19. Job — *93*
(71) Ibn Arabi Tells of John (the Baptist) — 94
Figure 20. John — *95*
(72) Ibn Arabi Tells of Zachariah — 96
Figure 21. Zachariah — *97*
(73) Ibn Arabi Tells of Elias — 98
Figure 22. Elias — *99*
(74) Ibn Arabi Tells of Luqmān — 100
Figure 23. Luqmān — *101*
(75) Ibn Arabi Tells of Aaron — 102
Figure 24. Aaron — *103*
(76) Ibn Arabi Tells of Moses: Manifold Wisdom — 104
Figure 25. Moses — *105*
(77) Ibn Arabi Tells of Moses: Rain and Youth — 106
(78) Ibn Arabi Tells of Moses: River Basket — 107
(79) Ibn Arabi Tells of Moses: Asiyah and Pharaoh — 108
(80) Ibn Arabi Tells of Khālid ibn Sinān — 110
Figure 26. Khālid — *111*
(81) Ibn Arabi Tells of Muhammad: Syzygy — 112
Figure 27. Muhammad — *113*
(82) Ibn Arabi Tells of Muhammad: Triads — 114
(83) Ibn Arabi Tells of Muhammad: 'The Opening' — 115
(84) Ibn Arabi Tells of Muhammad: The 'Last Name' of God — 116
(85) Ibn Arabi tells of the Substitute — 117

Prayers — **119**
(86) Ibn Arabi's Prayer: Sunday Evening — 120
(87) Ibn Arabi's Prayer: Sunday Morning — 121
(88) Ibn Arabi's Prayer: Monday Evening — 122
(89) Ibn Arabi's Prayer: Monday Morning — 123
(90) Ibn Arabi's Prayer: Tuesday Evening — 124
(91) Ibn Arabi's Prayer: Tuesday Morning — 125

(92) Ibn Arabi's Prayer: Wednesday Evening	126
(93) Ibn Arabi's Prayer: Wednesday Morning	127
(94) Ibn Arabi's Prayer: Thursday Evening	128
(95) Ibn Arabi's Prayer: Thursday Morning	129
(96) Ibn Arabi's Prayer: Friday Evening	130
(97) Ibn Arabi's Prayer: Friday Morning	131
(98) Ibn Arabi's Prayer: Saturday Evening	132
(99) Ibn Arabi's Prayer: Saturday Morning	133
Three Mystic Odes by Ibn Arabi	**135**
"Equal Worth of All Religions"	136
"Vision of the Divine Being"	138
"Apotheosis of the Human"	140
Appendix: "Art Bridges" by Shahid Alam	**141**
Source Notes	**145**
Bibliography	**149**
Supplementary Bibliography: Studies in Epiphanology by Martin Bidney	**153**

Introduction

God the All-Imaginer

(1) Situating Ibn Arabi in Context

In a masterly short treatise, *Imaginal Worlds: Ibn al-'Arabi and the Problem of Religious Diversity* (= *IW*), William C. Chittick shows how valuable for today's conflicted world is the penetrating and reconciling spiritual viewpoint of the famed religious thinker called by Sufi mystics "the Master of Masters." The God of Muḥyī al-Dīn ibn al-'Arabī (1165–1240) is one whose essential Being (*wujūd*) is unmanifest, unknowable by humans. The diversity of human imaginings of God arises from the diversity of the relations of the Forms that manifest Deity; of the states of spirit that receive the manifestations; of the historical and seasonal times that provide setting and context; of the types and degrees of human attention; of the goals of human imaginers; and of the disclosures that humans are capable of receiving (*IW* 157–162). The gods of belief are imaginative containers that shape and color what they hold (*IW* 262–263).

The animating breath enlivening the thought of Ibn Arabi is the single overpowering insight that God is the All-Imaginer. Simply by affirming this, one calls attention immediately to the startling novelty of the idea. In the prayers of Judaism, Christianity, and Islam we expect to hear the Deity praised for power, knowledge, and vastitude: He is the Omnipotent, Omniscient, Omnipresent. But Omnifingent? The All-Imagining? This we never hear.

Yet there are precedents and kinships. Ibn Arabi writes that "you are imagination": "everything which you perceive and concerning which you say 'This is not I,' is imagination, for *wujūd* [Essence, Being, God] is all imagination within imagination" (*Bezels of Wisdom*, qtd. *IW* 27). Chittick comments that "the term *imagination* refers to the greatest of all intermediate realities, which is the whole cosmos, or the Breath of the All-Merciful" (*IW* 26). You and I are imagination, and so is the entire imagined cosmos that we know through imagining, for we are each an imagining that we imagine to have been imagined by the Imaginer. In *The Four Zoas* poet and visual artist William Blake (1757–1827) envisions an Imaginer God embodied in four imagined Forms or Zoas, all co-present in the imagining or dreaming mind of every human being; and the chief of these is Urthona (Earth-owner) or Los the Eternal Prophet (Loss the Eternal Prophet [profit] = lose your unawakened self and find your true profit, your awakened imagination). In *Blake and Goethe* I have even experimented with the idea that if we interpret *Faust* as a sixty-year dream of the poet Goethe, four crucial characters in that dream-play—Faust (Passion), Mephistopheles (Intellect), Homunculus (Intuition), and the Eternal Feminine (Creative-Loving Imagining)—may be viewed as analogous to Blakean Zoas or Islamic Divine Names, manifestations of Divinity as it appears to our imagination.

In *The Marriage of Heaven and Hell* Blake writes, "Every thing possible to be believ'd is an image of truth" (8:38). In similar fashion, Ibn Arabi says, "People like us, who have an overview of all the stations and levels, distinguish from whence every individual speaks and discourses and recognize that each is correct in his own level and makes no errors" (*Meccan Openings* II.541.23 qtd. *IW* 140). The affinity is unmistakable.

Henry Corbin brings Ibn Arabi and Blake together in a convincing East-West affinity when he demonstrates their shared kinship with the influential theosopher Emanuel Swedenborg (1688–1772), in that all three visionaries interviewed imaginal, supernatural beings. Blake, in a crucial departure, turned much of Swedenborg's theosophy into psychology, as when he used "heaven" and "hell" simply to emblemize order and energy in the human psyche. But the centrality of imagination in religious experience for all three thinkers meant that they were alike in setting a high value on dreamlike visitations by beings who conveyed in perceptible form the intensity of supremely valued mental states or stages of awareness. It may be easy to satirize, as Blake did, the not always impressive utterance of a devil or angel to the Swedish quester. Yet Blake's long-term fruitful imaginative debates with Swedenborg, like the Ibn Arabi parallels that Corbin detects, show a depth of mental exploration that should not be discounted in evaluating Swedenborg's achievement as an important theosophic imaginer. Emerson's essay "Swedenborg; or, the Mystic" in his *Representative Men*, like the correspondence of Wassily Kandinsky and Arnold Schoenberg on Balzac's Swedenborgian vision in *Séraphita* (Taruskin 338–339), suggests the continuing life of a fruitful shared tradition, east and west.

Why then is Ibn Arabi still far less read in the West than he merits, or than one might reasonably have expected?

In standard Western histories of philosophy we hear of Avicenna (Ibn Sina) the Platonist, and we then hear of the supposed overshadowing of his Platonist "philosophy" by the later influence of Averroës (Ibn Rushd), the Aristotelian. This enables the Western student to place a clear, simple, broad periodizing of Islamic philosophy under a comfortably familiar three-traditions rubric. We can find clear Christian and Jewish parallels to the conventionally presented pattern of developing Islamic philosophy in an apparent yielding of predominance by the Platonist St. Augustine to the Aristotelian St. Thomas Aquinas, and of the overshadowing of the Platonist Philo by the Aristotelian-minded Maimonides. The trouble, though, as Corbin explains so well, is that our academic departments themselves are too narrowly focused to represent accurately the evolution of Islamic thought. The overly neat Judaism-Christianity-Islam parallels customarily drawn have distorted our outlook, for Islamic intellectual history is more richly complex than historians of (narrowly compartmentalized) philosophy have yet suspected.

Ibn Arabi did not chiefly intend to write systematic "philosophy" as Ibn Sina or Ibn Rushd attempted to do: rather, he is a *theo*sopher. Whereas a philosopher starts an investigation with doubt, a theosopher begins with God, and then tries to relate happenings in the created world to developments in the mind of Deity. (I follow Corbin in using the term "theosopher" and not "theosophist," for the latter word distractingly calls to mind the largely unrelated thinking of Blavatsky, Besant, and other thinkers of much more recent times.) Ibn Arabi is not the only thinker who suffers from this compartmentalizing, or departmentalizing, of study. Avicenna (Ibn Sina), too, is misrepresented when read only as a systematic practitioner of philosophy. Like Ibn Arabi, Ibn Sina was a visionary—one of the greatest, most influential of visionaries (see Corbin, *Avicenna and the Visionary Recital* passim).

Both questers were favored with mystical experiences, appearances, visitations, that were deeply central to their lives and teachings. Indeed, Ibn Arabi is the beneficiary—perhaps the culmination—of a powerful line of Platonist visionary discipleship stemming from Ibn Sina (Suhrawardi is a crucial mediator). For, just as Ibn Sina was not only a philosopher, so too Ibn Arabi was not only a theosopher:

philosophic subtlety and logical vigor are shown in his speculations on God the All-Imaginer, even though Ibn Arabi's religious mentors (prophets, messengers, visitants) generally meant far more to him than did either Arabic or Greek philosophers—with the one big exception of Plato (Addas 107–109). In fact, Ibn Arabi blends vision and reasoning as Plato did, and it is no accident that he praises Plato alone among systematic philosophers, calling him supreme among those enabled to "taste" all realms of Being with a direct imaginative and sensory immersion (see poem 18 below). We will see that in Ibn Arabi's world Platonic Forms have come alive—more alive, I would venture to say, than even Plato himself would ever have dreamed—in the guise of the Ninety-Nine Names of God. These might be called not Platonic Forms but post-Platonic *Forces*, no longer mere patterns or blueprint-plans, but summoning and guiding powers (see Corbin's analysis in *Alone with the Alone* [=*AwA*], which I've summarized).

Ibn Arabi enjoys a double triumph. Chittick calls him "probably the most influential thinker of the second half of Islamic history" (*IW* 1). Binyamin Abrahamov adds that the seminal idea of "the mutual reflection of God in the human being and the human being in God," along with "most of its ramifications," may be attributed to Ibn Arabi alone, while the theory "that each prophet represents an idea prevalent in the cosmos is also unprecedented" (Abrahamov 179). But it is equally true that Ibn Arabi maintained a continually lively dialogic exchange with nearly a dozen pre-eleventh-century Sufi visionary predecessors: "His disputes with some of them, even in dreams, show his profound absorption in the world of his predecessors, as if he believes all of them are in some way alive and hence available for discussion with him" (Abrahamov 171). In the history of theosophic thought and imagining, Ibn Arabi would seem to occupy a position analogous to that of J. S. Bach in the history of music: he sums up most of what had gone before in an unprecedentedly original synthesis that laid out prospects for the future.

(2) A Method of Epiphany Analysis

Gaston Bachelard (1884–1962), a groundbreaking thinker who, like Henry Corbin, was professor at the Sorbonne (see Jones for an overview of his work; Gaudin, ed., for samples), deserves to be likened to Ibn Arabi as another epoch-making theorist of imagination. He resembled the medieval Sufi sage in transcending categories, baffling the classifiers, and therefore resisting the "departmentalizing" of knowledge. Bachelard, unlike Ibn Arabi, thought of himself as chiefly a philosopher—specifically, a phenomenologist, or one who studies the structures of experience as we perceive it. Bachelard focused attention, as emphatically as Ibn Arabi had done, upon sensory-imaginative immediacy. For both of these thoughtful imaginers, tasting comes first, and reasoning follows. First we imaginatively shape our experience, and later we may speculate about its implications.

Bachelard studied what he called "reveries," or what literary analysts writing in English have come to call "epiphanies," imaginative revelations as they are experienced by readers of literature in any genre. An epiphany, as subjectively experienced, will be imaginatively and emotionally intense, will have wide implications, and will be mysterious, since the broad implications of an imaginative epiphany are typically out of all proportion to the brevity of the sudden, intense arousal. Like Ibn Arabi, Bachelard had an extraordinarily fertile poetic mind, and his writings about epiphanies often struck readers as an irreproducible, disconcertingly unpredictable kind of poetic writing, though ostensibly in prose. As an unhappy result of the seeming unclassifiability of his achievement, he has been badly shortchanged in the history of philosophy—as that field has all too often been narrowly defined. Literary critics, too (outside of France, where Jean-Pierre Richard, critic of Baudelaire and Mallarmé, proved a brilliant Bachelardian disciple), have failed to do him justice. A prolific writer like Ibn Arabi, he wouldn't fit into a "departmental" category.

In *Patterns of Epiphany* (1–21) and elsewhere (see the Supplementary Bibliography below), I systematized Bachelard's method into what I call an "epiphanology." I did this to show that he had, in fact, an implicit method and—more important—that any investigator could readily use it to illuminate moments of revelation in literature. Given the unusual visionary receptivity of those who fashion literary epiphanies, I suggested (following Bachelard) that such a person will likely fashion more than one of them. And the epiphanies framed by any distinctively talented imaginer will likely follow a recurrent pattern unique to that seer. Central to this formal, objectively discernible pattern will be the focus on a single element or combination of elements (earth, water, air, and fire), a recurrent pattern of motion, and a salient form or group of shapes, often semi-abstract or quasi-geometric. Bachelard noticed that, no matter how complex becomes the periodic chart used in science, the traditional quaternity of elements as the Greeks conceived it—earth, water, air, and fire—remains central to our deepest achievements of imaginative "reverie" or epiphanic revelation. Systematizing Bachelard, I further proposed that the element(s), motion pattern(s), and semi-abstract form(s) recurring in a given author's epiphanies should first be located in a vision of exceptional clarity and power. This exemplary vision would serve as the orienting paradigm. More attenuated or fragmented instances of the pattern could then be studied as relating to the paradigm.

The recurring criteria for an epiphanic image repertory—

namely element(s), movement pattern(s), and semi-abstract shape(s)—are not manifestations of pre-established laws or binding rules, but merely research tools. I use them because they have yielded results, revealing imaginative achievements that other methods failed to disclose in the work of (so far) over twenty writers. My Bachelardian method works well with Ibn Arabi, too, except that here I have not yet found any organizing paradigm that would exhibit all three epiphany components in one single unifying literary-imaginal moment. Therefore, we will simply proceed to examine them one by one, and will note, from time to time, their inter-implications. The components will prove, I think, to be psychologically and spiritually interrelated in valuably useful ways. The absence of a single "paradigm" may be a result of Ibn Arabi's modest wish to present himself chiefly as commentator on the Qur'an.

(3) Elemental Impulse: The Lover's Longing Sigh of Sadness

We are ready, then, to look at the three-part epiphany pattern of Ibn Arabi as shown in three sources: his *Meccan Openings* (or *Revelations*) offered in two volumes by Chittick (see Bibliography), *The Bezels of Wisdom* (bezels are gem settings, and the 27 prophets visited by Ibn Arabi on his tour of Heaven may be considered as "framing" unique jewels of insight into the Divine Being), and lastly *The Seven Days of the Heart,* a book of evening and morning prayers for one week. My monologue sonnets are based on these books, although additional Ibn Arabi sonnet-monologue cycles based on other works (e.g., the two volumes of *Meccan Revelations* edited by Chodkiewicz) could be envisioned. Henry Corbin, in *Alone with the Alone,* has headed me in the best direction at the start, for he has beautifully interpreted and accurately presented Ibn Arabi's revelation, in imaginative terms, of the origin of the world.

For Ibn Arabi, the origin of the world is an elemental epiphany of air. The breath which first brought creation into being was God's breath, and it was breathed out in *a sigh of longing for love*. Inspired, I feel sure, by this vision, Ibn Arabi wrote his own verses on the "religion of love" (see xliv below and 137, verses 13–15). "The pact" between the Divine and human natures "is born with the initial act of divine Love, which is the *Sigh of Sadness* [italics mine] compassionate with the nostalgia of the divine Names crying out for the beings who would will them" and lovingly assume them into their own natures (*AwA* 120). The Sigh of Sadness—in this we hear God's own melancholy yearning, in His lonely solitude, for beings whom He would create, in order that He might love and be loved by them. The creatures would become one with God's own breath and then—feeling the first deep Heavenly sigh re-arise within them—breathe it forth from their own hearts in responsive, com-passionate adoration of Him. Here is the central image of Ibn Arabi's Religion of Love.

In breathing out His sigh of longing for love, God caused the inclusive love-object, the cosmos, to appear, the created beings to exist, and thankful love to wake in each created being. I was writing my first responsive poem when I suddenly realized that, for Ibn Arabi himself, the happiest possible moment would occur when he felt so enfolded in the breath of God's love that he would feel his own responding, loving sigh vanish in the fullness of that primal breathing-forth of Being. "Who sighed to be revealed is comforted when I / Alive in that desire can vanish in that sigh" (cf. also poem 7).

Here I am commenting on Ibn Arabi's own declaration, in *Journey to the Lord of Power* (= *JLP*), that the seeker of God "will say unceasingly with every breath, 'My Lord, increase me in knowledge while the heavenly sphere turns by Your breath,' and let him strive that his Moment *be* His breath" (*JLP* 60). The "Moment," or *waqt*, as the commentator explains, "is an expression for your state in time" (*JLP* 99n40). The seeker makes his entire temporal life into God's own breath, vanishing in that enlivening sigh. *He will feel God breathe in his body all his life.*

Because the Primal Breath creates potentially responding Beloveds who will be thus also Lovers, it implies a breathing-forth of love in reply, and additionally a subsequent, and consequent, love dialogue that will be the animating force of Creation History. Originative epiphany indeed! It made the world, gave it shape, set it in motion. What is more, because God longs for love and needs it, and because we humans and the rest of the cosmos provide it, by loving we expand the Being not only of ourselves but of God. Henry Corbin, building on other Sufi traditions as well, ventures the comparison of Ibn Arabi's God to King Solomon and of us to the King's Beloved (*AwA* 251). But since the love-interchange promotes and expands the degree of fullness of Being in both lovers, it is equally true to say that we are Solomon and He is the Beloved (poems 11, 94). The lovers exchange their plentitudes of Being. As Ibn Arabi says in a poem, "By knowing Him, I give Him being" (qtd. *AwA* 124). The Qur'an, suggests Corbin, is in this regard something like "a variant of the Song of Songs" (*AwA* 251), a love letter sent and recited by Him and by us. Surely no imaginer of love has ever outdone this, and when I first read of it in Corbin I wanted to enter as fully as possible into the imaginative comprehension of the epic of love so engendered.

Corbin devotes an entire chapter to explaining how the love relation implicit in the Primal Breath of Love gives form and symmetric structure, in Ibn Arabi's view, to "The Opening," the first chapter or sura of the Qur'an, where the central message of that scripture is summed up in seven verses. There are three verses about God, then a verse about interchange, and finally three verses about humanity. It is a love relation embodied in a passionate dialogue (poem 83). "In this exchange, the Worshiper is the Worshiped; the Lover is the Beloved. Here no doubt we are far from the letter of the Koran as interpreted in the official cult, but we see how its spirit is understood when, in the private ritual of the Ṣūfī, the Koran is experienced as a version of the Song of Songs" (*AwA* 256).

The summoning breath of longing that began the world as love-dialogue reappears in many calls, cries, pleas, allied to sacred descents and gracious visitations. The sounds of yearning, of joyful-desperate imprecation, that travel through the upper and lower heavens vary and echo the theme of the initial elemental aery impulse, the Divine sigh, which revealed the sadness of One yearning to be known and treasured (*AwA* 113). God has ninety-nine Names derivable from the Qur'an, and Ibn Arabi explains that when God refers habitually to himself in the Qur'an as "We," this is not the "imperial we" or *pluralis maiestatis* but rather indicates the co-working of the Holy Names under the Divine superintendence (poem 49). Ibn Arabi portrays the Names as themselves engaged in "calling" or "summoning," intimating a "vocation." A Name of God is a Divine potential, or a rubric of related Divine potentialities; and when it calls, it summons you to realize what lies within you, your "vocation," in that hallowed, guided direction. When you feel able to respond deeply to the calling by the Name, you feel that it is your Name as well, at least until the next Name may summon you. Names are shared and exchanged (poem 42).

Sudden satisfaction in an unexpected achievement may reveal that a Divine Name has been newly manifested through your action. Thus, when you feel you have attained a startling enlightenment, an inner dawn or daybreak, you realize that the Divine Name "Cleaver of the Daybreak" allowed or empowered this to happen (poem 41). When you respond in a way that enables you to embody the Name that hailed, greeted, and summoned, you actualize or real-ize that Name, giving it an embodied reality in yourself, and are unified with God the Real in spiritual substance—again a lovers' mutual absorption, mutual incorporation or immentation, an exchange of canorous breathings of new-found harmony in the antiphon-canticle of spiritual love.

The love relation between the sighing God and the responding cosmos, or between Divine Name and receiving soul, is marvelously mirrored or echoed in the wedding of God to *every created object*. The world's objects, in their pre-created state, are already clamoring, begging, entreating God to give them reality in the created world! God is the Bridegroom, and the pre-created object is the prospective bride, who when granted the gift of creation will be the Beloved. The creating of the object that desires reality accomplishes the wedding between Creator and object. The marriage is perduring, and there is no possible divorce, for even if destroyed, the object will exist forever in the Imagination of God, perhaps under the rubric of the Name of Potentiality. The creation by God of any object echoes—without exception—His primal love song to the universe (poem 46).

The central epiphanic theme of the longing sigh is delightfully elaborated and multiplied in Ibn Arabi's dramatic allegory of the Council. Pre-created things wanted to achieve the actuality of Being in the world: they applied for marriage. They applied to the Names, who applied to the Name Powerful, who consulted his superior the Name Desiring, who at last convened the Council. Then the Name of Lordly Presence sent them forth and delegated the Name of Speaker to explain the relation between the things-to-be-created and the Names. We should note particularly that only the Name Desiring could convene the Council. We have here an allegory of the shapes and delegations and speakers of

Desire, again embodying the primal longing of the love-sigh (poem 45).

Names may summon us in many guises. Different Names are suited to appear on varied occasions. Khalid ibn Sinān, who hoped for prophethood but didn't get it, surely availed himself of the Name of Patience (poem 80). Ibn Arabi, who hopes for a direct tasting of the height and depth of Origin and object, prays that God invoke His Name of Forceful to aid the entreater (poem 90). The Three Angels who came to Abraham were bearers of His Names (poem 2). When we help to manifest the Names through thought and action, we amplify their Being and the Being of God Himself. As Abraham fed the angels, so we feed God with Being (poem 11). The Prophet Lot may have become dismayed by the difficulty of getting heard on God's behalf, but he teaches that the alleviator of fear is the hope that God may in time call us through a new Name that we had not thought might be ours, too (poem 64).

Adam enjoyed a glorious and quite unfallen relation to the calling Names. The Qur'an tells us that when Adam recited "the names," the angels bowed to him. Satan refused to bow—for why should fire bow to mere water and mud?—but as a creature of "essential fire" Satan may not have been truly an angel but only a jinn, a rebel daimon (I have written poems about this powerful episode from Qur'an 83:10–13: see *East-West Poetry* 30, 112–113). And Adam knew that God would love all His creatures, not despising one whose form was mud and water (poem 52). Many commentators assumed that it was the angels' names that Adam recited. But Ibn Arabi, true to Sufi tradition, tells us it was the Names of God Himself. Whatever we may do, our every action is our Name in action: when we know, recognize, envision a Divine Name we give it Being (poem 10). Because Adam knew all the ninety-nine Names, God said, according to a celebrated hadith account, that although the entire universe could not embrace Him, nonetheless "the heart of my faithful servant does embrace Me" (poem 9). We are not surprised that Ibn Arabi prays to learn the Names as Adam knew them (poem 96).

Following Muhammad, who is believed to have ascended to all the heavenly spheres and conversed with the prophets dwelling there, Ibn Arabi made his own heavenly ascent to converse with these advisors, who thereby came to serve for him a function analogous to that of the calling Names. And from these mentoring guides Ibn Arabi learns more about calls, entreaties, summonings—more voices animating the air of earth and heaven. From Job he learns that it is not impious to complain about suffering: we are made in God's image, and He is pained in the suffering of His forms (70). What is more, struggle is necessarily painful, and life is a struggle, or it should be: God loves the struggler more than the person of cloistered virtue, for the struggler has tasted more, sought more knowledge, and shown more patience (poem 36). Our "journey is based upon toil and the hardships of life, on afflictions and tests and the acceptance of dangers and very great terrors. It is not possible for the traveler to find in this journey unimpaired comfort, security, or bliss" (*JLP* 27).

From John the Baptist Ibn Arabi learns that if one's entreaty is to be granted, one should open it by mentioning the request, not oneself. John's father Zachariah did this when praying for a son, and Pharaoh's wife Asiya, who had converted to the faith of her former foster-child Moses, did this when praying on Pharaoh's behalf to the true God (poem 71).

From Zachariah himself Ibn Arabi learns that we don't have to beg for mercy, for it is everywhere. God manifested mercy to Himself in that first melancholy, longing, sighing breath which created everything (poem 72). There is a complexity, though, in the mercies we may be offered: one cannot always conform, equally or simultaneously, to the tendencies of all the Names that may be calling us. There may be a competition of mercies, a need to choose among them.

If, as seems appropriate, we group the varied summonings and disclosures regarding prayer, complaint, or entreaty as variants of the paradigmatic sigh of yearning which was at the same time the primal breath of creation, we may rightly view Ibn Arabi as an epiphanist of air. But not exclusively, by any means. He is, for instance, a visionary of fire as well. Importantly, one of his most telling fire metaphors relates integrally to the interrelation of fire and air. A big torch, he notes, may be put out by a sudden gust of wind while a protected votive candle burns on. Fear and trembling aren't always indicators of virtue but may instead betoken worry about the world-be lordly self. The taint of lordliness may generate the destructive winds that the small, modest fire of humility will avoid (poems 5, 32). In the same way, the fiery ruby is like the gracious radiance of God unobscured by the "lordliness" taint, which is likened to heavy iron (poem 19). The burning bush revealed to Moses the true guiding light, and that radiance itself was guided by the light of Muhammad. Ibn Arabi prays to God that he in turn may serve as a fiery light to guide others (poem 92).

It is even possible to temper the fires of hell in our thoughtful imaginings. The Qur'an mentions hell, so Ibn Arabi cannot deny its function. But he thinks that God may cool the flames of hell for sinners as he cooled the fires in which Abraham's father had tried to burn him alive after Abraham had wrecked the paternal gods (poem 69). A compassionate man here and always, Ibn Arabi informs us that Aaron told Moses it was not even necessary to burn the golden calf. Imagination makes progress, and the calf, though a less advanced way to envision a deity, was not wholly false but rather embodied an early stage or "station" of awareness (poem 75). In contrast, the non-punitive fires of Elias' flaming chariot emblemize awakened intellect, defeated lust (poem 73). It will be noticed that Ibn Arabi's epiphanic imagination favors not only breaths of love but moderated flames consistent with compassion and not destruction. Sometimes the peril of the flame is eliminated altogether and we focus only on the light, as when Ibn Arabi offers the metaphor of the illumination in a mirror, which makes vision possible but is not itself noticed—the kind of light by which we see, and which indeed in a sense we are (poem 37).

Water, similarly, is viewed as doubly comforting—refreshing and protective—and so it was for Moses in youth and in maturity. When this prophet feels the gentle rain descending as in his boyhood, he is revisited, in what readers of English may deem a nearly Wordsworthian fashion, by an awareness of youth returned (poem 77). Indeed, Ibn Arabi posits that the children murdered by Pharaoh did not entirely die: their spirits remained, lending treasures of youthful insight when they took up their abode within the mind of Moses (poem 76). The reed basket in which Moses was carried on the Nile is an emblem of his human nature divinely guided on the waters of life-experience (poem 78).

In perhaps the most memorable of his water metaphors, Ibn Arabi explains that our spirit is like water, which takes on the shape and color of its container: we know God to the extent to which we know ourselves, according to the kind and level of knowledge we have been enabled to contain at any given moment (poem 54). Indeed, Ibn Arabi claims to have learned from Muhammad the prime importance of what he calls the "Last Name" of God—the one we've most recently learned, whose level we've most lately attained. It is this Name that prays in us and with us, and which gives the water of our spirit its form and color. The cup, as container, is a metaphor of conditioned belief (poem 24). All our beliefs are conditioned, they are all colored cups. No doctrine should be scorned: monasticism, though not prescribed in the Qur'an, shows an ardent will to serve the

Highest, and thus may be approved and not condemned (poem 59). Those who turned away from the instructions of Noah had a knowledge that was incomplete, both of self and God: the cure for this, as for all relative ignorance, is more knowledge, both of the immanent and transcendent nature of the Creator (poem 54). Those who refused to follow the Prophet Hūd will nonetheless attain mercy, for morning light is everywhere (poem 61). A belief is a metaphor, and every such act of imagination requires respect within its clearly comprehended context of origin (poem 13).

Milk and wine are other epiphanic liquids whose benign effects are allegorized. Milk is a symbol of knowledge (poem 67)—widely available, nourishing, beneficent—and Ibn Arabi dreamed of being immersed in milk up to his chest (poem 17). Wine is considered from three angles. The tasting of wine is like the encounter with a friend. The drinking of wine is like the meeting with a messenger (of God, or of holy wisdom). The quenching of thirst by wine is like the companionship of a prophet (poem 8). "Tasting" itself is Ibn Arabi's word for the concreteness of lived experience, prior to all reasoning or analysis. We reason in concepts mediated by words, which are failed adequations to tasting in both sensory and spiritual life, misleading applications of analogies. As Al-Ghazāli famously pointed out, "The difference between God's attributes and ours is greater than the difference between the pleasure of sexual intercourse and the sweetness of sugar" (paraphrased by Treiger 52). Beliefs, even Names, are like "knots," each binding something to secure it, but each also capable of aiding in an imprisoning constriction (poems 3, 13, 24). Knots are a danger for the taster (poem 16): when belief constricts direct experience, it is time to advance to a higher stage or waystation. As the name of the Prophet Shu'aib means "diverge" or "ramify" (branch out), so we must keep in mind the multiplicity as well as the bounds of our beliefs (poem 63).

The knotted fibers let us make a neat transition to Ibn Arabi's metaphorics of earth, including the lessons to be learned from caves and roots. A cave should signify withdrawal into God, not an escape from life. The Qur'anic prayer "My Lord! Increase me in knowledge" (20:114) is a request for more experience, not less. Reclusion is not required, for you have a cave within you (poem 18). Physical retreats are not forbidden, however: they are encouraged. The hard but recommended discipline of a retreat seems intimated in "Deification of the Human," a poem where Ibn Arabi speaks of foot wounds in the wilderness. He has devoted a treatise, *The Four Pillars of Spiritual Transformation*, to the value of cultivating, in contemplative solitude, a training through silence, seclusion, hunger, and vigilance. One may even acquire, in a place of retreat, a newly born or "substitute soul," which later visitors to that holy place may see (poem 85).

A most beautiful epiphany invoking the power of a nourishing centrality in the earthly emblem of the root is that in which Ibn Arabi portrays three metaphoric prostrations. Shadows bow to light they cannot see. Reeds will bend to wind they only feel. Best of all, the human heart bows to the unseen root of grounded Being (poem 22). Indeed, a low bow nobly recalls the descent of Angel Gabriel to earth, so that through angelic ministry Muhammad might be given the Qur'an (poem 12).

Additional earth-revelations are those of the horn and the mustard seed. The horn, resembling the judgment trumpet, is a metaphor of imagination itself, with God at the top where the mouthpiece would be, and with the world of physical thing-metaphors in the widened area below (poem 6). As the horn-tone descends, the mustard seed arises. Much loved by the Christian evangelists (Matt. 13:31, 17:20; Mark 4:31; Luke 13:19, 17:6), the mustard seed is also the vehicle of one of the wisest teachings of Luqmān, a prophet known for wisdom (poem 74).

In Matthew, for example, we learn that the mustard seed represents the Kingdom of Heaven, rising from small beginnings to become a large plant where birds gather, and that faith as small as a mustard seed will generate in the believer the willpower to move mountains by command. From Luqmān Ibn Arabi learns that the mustard seed represents the Divine nature: the sown, unsprouted, essential nature of each person is known to God, Whom it rejoices in that heavenly knowledge while it is still beneath the earth or in a state of potential. It then rises to rejoice the earth as well as the heaven when the potential is made real and the seed unfolds.

An earthly being more problematic for the interpretive imagination is the ram in the story of Abraham's non-sacrifice of his son. Before carrying out God's command to take his son with him on a journey, as Ibn Arabi explains, Abraham had dreamed he was offering up a ram in the son's form. The dream-truth was that Abraham would soon kill a ram. The distorted apparent implication, introduced by Satan, was that the son would be involved in the act of slaying. Dreams reveal, but may distort what is revealed. The human imagination comes from God, but will need to seek ever greater propinquity to that Source, in order to gain clear understanding (poem 57). "When Muhammad said, 'All men are asleep and when they die they will awake,' he meant that everything a man sees in this life is of the same kind as that which one sleeping sees; in other words an apparition that requires interpretation" (*BW* 196–197).

Most important in the realm of earth-metaphor, Ibn Arabi is fond of the metaphor of the *barzakh*, meaning bridge or isthmus. Everything we know is only part of the truth, a metaphoric bridge between the unknown Essential Being and us. The whole created world, even the image or conception we have of God Himself, is like an image in a mirror—a bridge linking the unknowable, unmanifest (incomparable, essential) nature of God and His manifest nature which may be validly if somewhat distantly approached through metaphor. Look into the mirror: your image is both there in the mirror and not there in the mirror (poem 39). We need objects to witness that an unknown God created them, and objects need us to witness that they bear witness (poem 40). Metaphors are imaginings, and the ontologic status or degree of reality ascribable to anything imagined always has to be ambiguous or indefinite because it conveys knowledge that is only partial. The only things we know about God are our beliefs about Him, beliefs which are imaginings. These imaginings are metaphors of the Real, but they cannot wholly disclose the Real since they tell nothing of the unmanifest aspect of the nature of God.

Importantly, since we are created in God's likeness, and since God has both manifest and unmanifest aspects to His Nature, so do we: metaphors are bridges to the unknowable part of ourselves, too. I especially admire this part of Ibn Arabi's envisioning of us. Part of myself will forever be unknown, unmanifest, to me. An even number is a metaphor of likeness, of metaphor itself. An odd number is a metaphor of unlikeness, of the unmanifest that is within. Our symmetric, two-part body is even. But our five-fingered hand is odd. Ninety-nine is odd—for that is the number of the metaphoric names of a God the unimaginable aspect of Whose Being is unmanifest (poem 48).

Night is a beneficent bridge. It is far from being Void and should never bring on despair. It is dark compared to day, but bright compared to void or non-being or nothingness. We see the image of Night, we imagine it, and it therefore in part illuminates (poem 44). Time is a metaphor of God. Day is a metaphor of revealing. Night is a metaphor of expectant interval (poem 31). But the darkness of our sublunary world also admits of another metaphoric emblem, a less advantageous, even a threatening one, that must be excised by anyone ambitious of emulating Muhammad's upward-guiding example. This is the speck of impurity that the three angels removed from the Prophet's heart when they excised it on the mountain, before replacing the purified heart, new-freshened with a cooling liquid, so that Muhammad could arise in a condition worthy of one who would speak the word of God. It is for such a removal of the blood-speck of Satan that Ibn Arabi prays (poem 86).

And who is Satan? As the one who tried, during the temptations in the desert, to compel Jesus to believe in him, Satan becomes for Ibn Arabi the metaphor of all compulsion in religion. The Qur'an (2:256) strictly forbids all compulsion in religion. Beliefs are like knots, but they are knots we ourselves have tied so as to anchor or to hoist ourselves to a vantage point of higher, wider view. When somebody else ties the knots and fetters us with them, they become a prison, which is the opposite to valid religions. These latter must forever be rooted in the freedom of imagining (poem 28).

Crucial to the metaphorics of earth as the site where we joyfully begin our lives in prayer is the love of God for every human being, for we are each His Godly shrine of moistened mortal clay, revered even by the angels if not by rebel Satan. One individual embodied human soul is not only God's temple, but a vast congregation assembled for prayer in that temple! The soul is an imam leading in devotional homage the assembly of all the organs and faculties of the physical-spiritual miracle that is our body. Within the corporeal shrine will arise a harmonious hymn of uncountable voices. In this epiphany of worship Ibn Arabi has unquestionably attained one of his supreme poetic triumphs (poem 12).

Before leaving the topic of earth epiphanies, we should try to do justice to the guiding metaphor of bezels, or gem settings (poem 52). When Ibn Arabi toured the heavenly spheres he interviewed the prophets dwelling there, and each man served as the framer of a gem, a flash of insight (cf. poems 19, 92). I particularly enjoy picturing gem settings of gold, prized for their craftsmanship among the jewel connoisseurs of medieval Persia, for such bezels bring to mind the extraordinary epiphany manifested by goldsmiths to poet Mevlana Rumi (1207–1273), often viewed as Ibn Arabi's theosophically-minded parallel or counterpart. When Rumi's longtime spiritual comrade Shams (literally, Sun) was evidently murdered with the connivance of the poet's jealous son, Rumi could not consider mourning as appropriate, either on his own behalf or that of Shams. Rather, Rumi went to the bazaar and, as he walked among the goldsmiths' booths, was entranced by the harmonies of the delicate clinking hammers (which always make me think of the Balinese gamelan ensembles that later inspired composer Claude Debussy). Rumi seized one of the goldsmiths, an old friend, by the arm and the two of them began a whirling dance. Thus the man, Salahuddin Zarkub, who was to become Rumi's next and lasting spiritual comrade, is said to have participated in the founding moment of the Mevlevi order of whirling dervishes (Schimmel, *Rumi's World* 18–23).

We have looked at the elemental aspect of Ibn Arabi's world of epiphanies and noted the primacy of air in the primal breath of longing, and also the fertility of invention in the emblematic use of fire, water, and earth—all brought into the poetic service of a compassionate and gracious love-dialogue, the canticle of Creator and creature, each of these enriching the other's plenitude of Being. We should now examine two other observable components of Ibn Arabi's epiphanic image repertory: the recurrent motion pattern and the predominant type of semi-abstract shape or configuration of space.

(4) Motion Pattern: Nano-second Alterations

The chief pattern of movement in the most memorable epiphanies of Ibn Arabi is genuinely startling and unprecedented in my experience of reading. It consists of an unending stream or sequence of alterations, each lasting but a fraction of a micro-second. No other epiphanic motion I have yet encountered is quite so relentlessly dynamic, not even Elizabeth Barrett Browning's recurrent epiphanies, in her epic *Aurora Leigh*, of the turning of stones to fire (Bidney *PE* 172–196).

Split micro-second transitions of awareness characterize the mind of God Himself. Ibn Arabi bases this idea in large part on the Qur'anic statement that "each day" the Lord is "upon some task" (55:29). Since "days" are vastly different, and infinitely faster, in God's life than in ours, Ibn Arabi takes this to mean that some *new* task is undertaken each moment or micro-moment, and since the conceiving power of the Almighty is so infinitely powerful, the variety of tasks must be endlessly diverse and unfathomably rapid. The "tasks are the states" of the "creatures, who are the loci for the existence of the tasks within them, since it is within them that He creates those states perpetually. Hence no state can remain for two moments" (Chittick, *The Sufi Path of Knowledge* 99). The speed, at times, of our dream life is a psychological metaphor of this unintermittent, unpredictable transformation. The chameleon is the supreme symbolic embodiment of it among earthly creatures (poem 15). To be in Paradise, and to face God always, is to experience the never-ending lightning-speed mental activity posited by Ibn Arabi.

How different from the usual ways of representing Heaven! More often, we associate the dead with the phrase "Rest in peace," and people who utter that tired phrase appear to be wishing, desiring, and requesting permanent tranquillity for the departed. But Ibn Arabi is a promoter and admirer of vigorous activity: we recall his depiction of life as struggle—and as perplexity, too, for freedom baffles (poem 36). Ibn Arabi's elated awareness of the paradisal life as one of superhumanly swift energies operating in ever-altering directions gives new vividness, I think, to his insightful metaphor of the "King's Command," a mysterious royal (Heavenly) call to heed some entirely unfamiliar appearance of God-communicated insight, a disorienting moment that may be deeply unsettling to us and to those who, in our immediate earthly situation, may look at us with surprise and discomfort (poem 38).

Let us examine in more detail the visual features of this recurrent epiphany of God in lightning-swift perceptive and ever-alert awareness. The darting chameleon seems to comprehend this better than any other creature, through in dreams we attain our own intimation of chameleonic thought (poem 15). In paradise, God additionally practices nano-second approaches and withdrawals, heightening still further the sensation of unending novelty. Such intensive activity shows, in dismaying contrast, what an arbitrarily willful spirit-veiling the state of human boredom can be (poem 20).

The culminating epiphany in this series, I would venture, is Ibn Arabi's explanation of the distinction between our earthly and heavenly conditions. On earth, we inhabit a body that looks much the same throughout the day, while our mental life is filled with diversities, including distractions. In paradise, our mental life will take on the steadiness, the constancy, that our bodily appearance has throughout the day on earth: we will have our mind solely focused on God, enjoying an understanding of Him that is barely possible here. But in heaven our outer appearance, signaling our changing nature momently renewed, will alter continually (poem 26). We will of course need to be specially empowered to endure this. But the Qur'an assures that a merciful God gives us no more than we can bear, that God will not "tax any soul beyond its scope" (7:42)—and in our earthly life, as well, when by the Name of Forgiveness we are led away from perilous areas of thought, we may be granted analogously overwhelming riches of Name-revelation, which we are mercifully taught to master (poem 53).

In the midst of this whirl, we shall be steadied in Paradise, as we are already calmed to a significant degree on earth, by the awareness that the presence of God is constant, the underlying basis of all change. God's presence is veiled by physical things that appear to alter only when we consider them apart from Him, regarding them merely as "things"—for thinghood by itself will disappoint (poem 87). When the Qur'an says, "Everything will perish save His countenance" (28:88), it means that only what tells of a thing's relation to its Maker survives (poem 3). Thus, in formulating the motion component of Ibn Arabi's epiphanic pattern, we should say that a presentation of nano-second alterations goes together with an awareness of an inalienable, inseparable counterpart—the abiding nature, manifest and unmanifest, of the Maker of time.

In sum: the second major component of Ibn Arabi's epiphanic imagining, namely the pattern of movement, is as aptly suited to his Religion of the Lover's Breath of Longing as the elemental predominance of the yearning-and-creative breath of air that we have studied. Extreme alertness to the changes in thought, sensation, and feeling experienced by the one we love, rapid as they may be, is beautifully and instructively counterbalanced by the steadiness of our faithful adherence, the attachment we feel to one we love. Everything said about love in the preceding sentence may apply to both spouse and God. God is our steadiness amid every fluctuation of the heart: His Mercy will always outweigh His Judgment (poem 58) in order that the heart be advanced and its progress rewarded (poem 27).

(5) Semi-Abstract Images: Line, Point, and Plane

Turning, lastly, to the third chief component in the epiphany pattern of Ibn Arabi, we ask: how is space configured in his imaginal world? There is a threefold answer: in line, point, and plane. Space is arranged in spiritual levels variously imagined in a spatial framework. Our lives in physical and in spiritual space are parts of an unending journey: "Know that since God created human beings and brought them out of nothingness into existence, they have not stopped being travelers" (*JLP* 27). "Each person has a path that no one else but he travels," a path which comes "to be through the travelling itself" (*Contemplation of the Holy Mysteries* 5). We learn of "waystations," suggesting points of temporary halting in a traveler's journey: so in a poem with overtones of a pilgrimage Hafiz (ca. 1320–1389) writes, "Travelers know the roadways; / Acquainted, they, with posting stations" (Bidney, *PWTR* 2). But the waystations are points on the way to a fuller awareness of God's Light (*SPK* 2-21), so the stopping places could just as well be points on a vertical line. In the progress toward Light, the moon is a metaphor of limited disclosure, the sun a symbol of full disclosure (or full*er*—since the knowledge of God that comes to us by the power of the Sun is still seventy times veiled [poem 14]). Ibn Arabi prays to be content with the stages and stations through which he passes, keeping focused on the Bright One through varied light and dark, in emulation of the moon (poem 98). Patience is a waystation, which can become a longer-lasting abode when receptivity is increasingly rewarded (poem 23).

Perhaps we may then call every waystation a mode of patience, or every patience a waystation. Job, God, and the recording angels all show patience: misery, furthered by impatience, can be a veil, so the discarding of it may be a revelation or un-veiling (poem 61). A touching and unusual perspective on the need for patience comes from Ibn Arabi's speculation that God as Lover may postpone the fulfilment of a wish because he wants to hear the beautiful entreaty of His beloved (poem 66). Here again we are strikingly reminded that we are learning the Religion of Love: our love for each other is the best key to its interpretation. When Ibn

Arabi portrays reason, habit, and imagination as three talismans, he may be seeing them as ascending waystations (poem 33). The fact that Adam accepted God's Trust—when nothing else in the Universe was ready to do so (Qur'an 33:72)—commits us, in our role as viceregents of His, to strive continually to perfect our understanding of Him at ever higher levels (poem 9).

Because we think of progress as a rising, we may hope to see ourselves as most importantly occupying points on a line of ascent or elevation: God directs the earnest quester always on the "straight path" (Qur'an 1:5). But because God's Face is everywhere you look (Qur'an 2:115), all paths that lead to Him are straight: each is cor-rect and recti-linear in being rightly di-rected (poem 30). Motion, progress—along a path of whose ultimate straightness perhaps God alone will be aware—must always be crucial: poverty is a metaphor of spiritual freedom, since the rich are imprisoned by cramping, crippling concern for what they think to be their wealth (poem 29). Upward movement is prized: Jesus raised the dead. We do this too when we bring souls to the Light (poem 66).

But the complexity of the spiritual world adds subtlety to the idea of linear direction in movement. "Man was ever hasty" (Qur'an 7:11); we pray too hastily, and misguided prayers can set us off toward goals unworthy of our movement in those directions (poem 32). Ibn Arabi observes on awaking that it takes time for "lines of light" to come together in clear physical images before the drowsy eyes: this he takes to emblemize the gradual shaping of spiritual awakening, as well (poem 47). When the Prophet, in Heaven, attains a position only two bows' length from God (Qur'an 53:9), the unified circle of God's Nature may appear split by a line into two semicircles when viewed by Muhammad's human perception, yet at the same time the curvatures, seen as aligned, are uniting the two aspects of God's working through the connecting line of the Prophet. God inclines while Muhammad rises (poem 50)—and with equal fitness it may be said that when the biblical Enoch rose, God descended (poem 55). These are aspects of the same motion, involving the symbolic alignment of two curvatures, or two straight lines. We must be alert to the changing uses of point, line (curved or straight), and level or plane in the metaphors of Ibn Arabi.

An extraordinarily beautiful alignment occurs in Ibn Arabi's imagining of what I call a "syzygy" (poem 81), which is the lucky lineup of three heavenly bodies—in heaven-gazing, generally sun, moon, and earth. God, man, and woman are aligned in love. In order that God not become jealous when man sees His divine image in woman, God purifies man's image of woman so that His own image will be seen there. Love, purified by God, sees woman in God. All three, so configured in metaphorical alignment, become metaphors for the Divine nature. Ibn Arabi enjoys this alignment so much that he varies it in the poem commenting on Muhammad's professed love for prayer, perfume, and woman. Perfume, a masculine noun, is flanked by two feminine nouns, prayer and woman. In the same way, Essence (or Cause), man, and woman can be lined up so that a masculine noun is flanked by two nouns of feminine gender—the same FMF alignment Ibn Arabi had set up earlier (poem 82). Ibn Arabi likes to imagine alignments of triads: when the Prophet Ṣāliḥ asks for, and is granted, three days of mercy, it is suggested that these may represent Essence, Will, and Word, the threefold means by which we make known our response to the Love of God (poem 62).

All reality is in God: though we increase His plenitude of Being in reciprocating His love, love itself is the treasure that is His in its origin and nature and being. God is Himself the treasure that wanted to be revealed and loved, a desire that motivated the entire Creation to take place. Every manifested treasure should therefore be grateful for its existence; and every treasure will be more cherished the greater is our love for the One Who is both the treasure and its revealer (poem 43). Solomon-God imagined the Cosmos-Beloved who would be his dialogic partner in Love. We ought therefore to be modest in not claiming too much merit or self-subsistence. God's are "the most beautiful names" (Qur'an 20:8), and we perceive the Beauty of God by means of Modesty, which is a beauty of character (poem 21). Religion itself is a code of Courtesy, and Courtesy is a kind of taste or beauty of character (poem 35). Without God the self is dream, and Ibn Arabi therefore prays for self-nihilation (poem 89). Let the self be nihilated as the mountain of Mosaic revelation was crushed (Qur'an 7:143, poem 95)!

Even if the prayer be answered and the self nihilated, the soul that is thereby purified to see God does not cease to manifest Him. Yet there remains a degree of distinction between God and His manifestation in that purified soul. For this reason, Ibn Arabi argues, it shows more Courtesy, more taste and beauty of character such as God Himself embodies, not to say, "I am the Truth," as did the pious Al-Hallaj (poem 11) or Ibn Yazid (poem 19). Corbin links the type of Courtesy we should cultivate to that of the medieval *fedele d'amore,* the courtly lover who wrote heart-songs of troubadour imagining (*AwA* 100–101, 142–144). Only by such Courtesy can we ward off the taint of lordliness in the created soul. We possess inalienable freedom—compulsion in religion is Satanic—but we mirror God, we freely serve our fate (poem 56). And even though we and God in our love relation continually and freely exchange Being, nonetheless our freedom interacts with God's freedom in ways that we cannot know, and should not wish to know, completely. Therefore God was right to rebuke the Prophet 'Uzair (sometimes equated to Ezra, e.g., *Bezels* 163–171) for overeagerness to learn of destiny (poem 65). Joseph dreamed, but so do we all—and all the time—for God's world is what He imagines, and His Essence is forever unmanifested, although His attributes appear in created likenesses such as we are (poem 60). In sum, courtesy is required by the distance between God and the created soul, situated as they are on *different ontological levels or planes.*

The two tautened bowstrings are aligned: as our aspiration ascends, Mercy comes down to meet it, and the two levels coincide in a shared path. The wooded hills praised King David, and Mercy inclines to grant harmony to us (poem 68). Because Pharaoh's wife Asiya mercifully protected and served the young Moses, it became possible for Moses later to convince Pharaoh to convert to faith in God before that otherwise hapless monarch died (poem 79). Ibn Arabi prays to receive the kind of merciful comfort that the parents of John the Baptist felt upon the birth of their Prophet-son (poem 88). The supreme degree of Mercy is Pardon. God forgave Jonah; God is in everyone, so to forgive anyone at all does God a favor (poem 69). Ibn Arabi prays that God may pardon him as He pardoned Noah, Jonah, Job, and Moses, and that He will grant the knowledge that turns the spirit from the changeful to the Source (poem 93). Mercy culminates when Spirit inclines or bows in Pardon, and victory is won by the Religion of Love.

Following the example of God, Who by His primal breath created, and now continues to create, a world of beings He can love and be loved by, Ibn Arabi's power of imagination summons forth spiritual families of guides and fellow seekers. He tells us that a woman who was also a visionary presence for him, Fátima of Córdoba, on meeting Ibn Arabi's mother, saw an image of the Prophet Muhammad, an auspicious sign of a special destiny and divine appointment for her son (poem 4). White-robed Moses and Aaron visited Ibn Arabi in his retreat (poem 91). In the final poem of my collection, Ibn Arabi tells, in the last of his fourteen prayers, of his thanks for seven gifts on the seventh day: he has received the same favors as were given to Abraham's angel, Moses, Jesus, Adam, Noah, Isaac, and Jacob—and it was the Prophet Muhammad who made possible the working of this visionary transformation granted to him (poem 99).

We are ready to summarize what the analysis of Ibn Arabi's epiphanic patterns has now shown us. The life of imagination, as taught us by God Omnifingent, the All-Imaginer, consists in loving exchanges between spiritual beings physically manifested—a dialogue or colloquy that allows messages to travel between them in both directions, like the inhaling and exhaling of breath. It is the unity of sensual tasting and spiritual delectation, both expressing a love that is alert to endlessly rapid and unpredictable changes of awareness while being grounded in the rootedness of constancy and fidelity. This imaginal love travels on the right path through levels or stations of awareness—horizontally, vertically, or with the aid of bendings in our travel-path and inclinations or bowings in mercy. The changeful variety of these manifested metaphors of direction means that the "straightness" or spiritual progression of our journeying may not be wholly perceptible by us at a given point, or at any point. But as confident pilgrims we may surely cultivate the Qur'anic faith that we "shall journey on from plane to plane" (84:19). The Qur'an—the scripture the Prophet recited but also the one written in our hearts—is a canticle of Love, a Solomonic poem.

(6) My Dramatic Monologue Sonnet Form

To affirm God as All-Imaginer leads us straight to the heart of Ibn Arabi, the most overpoweringly impressive systematic thinker of Sufism, or mystical Islam. Himself a supremely fertile imaginer, Ibn Arabi—not surprisingly—wrote memorable poetry. The following brief lyric excerpt (see Source Notes xliv below) would even make a suitable motto for his entire visionary life:

Boundless Love

> My heart could any form at all put on:
> A scholar-cloister, meadow with gazelle,
> A pagan temple, pilgrim kaaba-spell,
> The Torah tablet, the revered Qur'an.
> I hold to Love's religion: where his steed
> May turn I ride, and Love permit to lead.

Because Love Unbounded is God, Ibn Arabi emulates the Divine example by imagining himself as partaking from those endless and varied colored cups which contain faith in the gods of belief. By embracing all believers in their roles of adoration, Ibn Arabi the poet embodies and demonstrates a love for all who seek the Highest with heart and soul. He sighs with longing on behalf of each of us.

Though as a spokesman of Love's religion Ibn Arabi is known best for his prose writing, this too is inherently poetical, filled with an exemplary richness of metaphor. I have hoped to pay him adequate homage as thoughtful imaginer by responding in lyric verse. My mode of tribute is the dramatic monologue sonnet, representing Ibn Arabi as conveying each revelation in a spoken poem.

The lyrics of homage I offer are ninety-nine, the traditionally accepted number of the sacred Names of God as given in the Qur'an. While writing, I became increasingly delighted to realize that by focusing on Ibn Arabi's metaphors, his emblematic images or pictures, we find a wealth of parables rivaling that of Jesus. A parable may be viewed as an image in narrative action, the depiction of a physical (or, less often, conceptual) object that, as it moves through the narrator's thought, conveys a fabular message. Jesus' parable of the mustard seed, recounted in Matthew, Mark, and Luke, is fully comparable to Ibn Arabi's parable on the same theme. I offer fifty-one verse parables to pay tribute, in lyric form, to this important—and not yet adequately recognized—spiritual phenomenon of Ibn Arabi as supreme Sufi parabolist. My lyrics are only a sampling of possibilities: one interpreter, in a single short book, can provide little more than intimations.

In poems 52 through 84, I again focus on imagery while commenting on each of the interviews that Ibn Arabi, following the example of the heaven-tour of Muhammad, conducted with the prophets on the planets. My poetical comments on the visionary sojourns do not always coincide in focus with what Ibn Arabi or his translator-commentator R. W. J. Austin found doctrinally most important. The theosopher's chapters are richly and freely associative, and at times I found a subordinate or digresssive paragraph more stimulating than what might be deemed the central lesson. None of my poems is a versification of Ibn Arabi's text. They are all written with the imaginative dream-mind, and though each one begins with a source in Ibn Arabi (identified in the Source Notes), additional links or bridges may be my own interpolations, usually remembered from other passages by Ibn Arabi. Freedom in choice of focus and in mode of elaboration distinguishes the response of a poet from the systematic commentary of an exegete. After using transitional poem 85 to show Ibn Arabi's faith in the efficacy of retreat for spiritual cultivation, in poems 86 through 99 it is vividness of image that I favor once again in responding to Ibn Arabi's week of prayers at morn and eve.

I invented a new kind of iambic pentameter sonnet (fourteen-line poem) for all the monologues in this collection. The rhyme pattern in the opening two quatrains (the octet) is usually ABCD ABCD (though occasionally a couple of the letters will be switched if the thought seems to require it). The two final three-liners (the sestet) have their rhymes distributed in a pattern allowing for multiple options, as often happens within the tradition of Petrarchan sonnet-writing (examples: EFF EFE, or EEF FGG). The novelty of my experimentation in the sonnet genre is found in the

ABCD ABCD rhyming. "Deferred gratification rhymes," as we might call them, do not call attention to themselves and thus may let us think of Ibn Arabi as mulling things over in the first eight lines before he is ready to formulate the concluding insight he will offer. "Immediate gratification rhyming" then strives, in the final six lines, to shape the well-pondered conclusions with a more traditional and proverb-like concision and lyric beauty. Because the "free verse" practiced widely by anglophone poets today has little kinship with the aesthetic mentality of medieval Islamic writers, I chose instead a form that would have the features the earlier imaginers admired: metrical regularity and intricate, relatively consistent patterns of rhyming. In this way I hope to have paid homage both to the poetic fertility of Ibn Arabi and to the golden era of verse-writing in which he lived.

(7) Ibn Arabi's Three Mystic Odes

Additionally, I offer three mystic odes by Ibn Arabi (*Mystische Texte* [= *MT*]), which I have newly translated from the German of M. Horten (1912), who rendered them (evidently adding his own titles to the poems) from the Arabic originals (1240). Horten uses no meter but only prose with no line-breaks. I have made each verse a couplet of two alexandrines or hexameters with twelve syllables each, a form close to the one called *beit* often used e.g. by the Persian-language masters Rumi and Hafiz. At the beginning and end of the central poem I have made some three-line verses to accommodate the unusual richness of thought and imagery. Rhymes are omitted, for I could not feel where they ought to be, given the absence of a verse original to work with. However, Horten is scrupulous in his prose rendering, often giving one or more alternative word choices and explanations in brackets and appending, in interpretive discussions, a number of Ibn Arabi's own notes on both literal and allegorical meaning. Incorporating some of these notes, and of Horten's extrapolations from them, I would like to show briefly how the three mystic odes relate to Ibn Arabi's worldview and epiphany pattern.

The philosophic and poetic center of "Equal Worth of All Religions" may be found in verses 13–15, the same ones rephrased in "Boundless Love," Annemarie Schimmel's version, translated and cited above (xliv). The Religion of Love, beginning with God's primal breath, a sigh of longing to love and to be loved in return, is embodied here in Ibn Arabi's expression of eagerness to enter the mental states of those who worship the varied gods of belief at the different stages or stations of human imaginings of God, Whose Essence is unknowable. "Let thy soul be as matter for all forms of all beliefs" (*AwA* qtd. 119). All religions are of equal worth when considered as earnest human strivings toward the Highest. They are colored cups, containers of faith as we shape it in the various stages and stations we are capable of attaining.

The poet begins by begging the doves of Divine intimation to cease reminding him so painfully of separation from Deity. Their sighing love-moan (3) echoes the breath of tristful yearning breathed out by God Himself in the love religion of the poet. Even the spirits in the tamarind marsh (4) have contact with the still-hidden soul of the poet only by way of his four constitutive physical elements, each called a foundation or pillar of his material being. These higher spirits surround the longing lover, even as Muhammad the Prophet, the perfected soul, walked around the holy kaaba stone (8): thus what is loftier will raise up what is lower. A metaphor of the Muslim's pilgrimage to Mecca enters with the reference to the symbolic throwing of little stones (6) to shoo away the devils, or thoughts unworthy of the striver: the pilgrim-custom intimates the theme of progression, of Meccan pilgrimage, betokening the Sufi journey past the varied waystations to farther goals and higher levels. Ibn Arabi's reservations regarding the worth of the Kaaba stone (9) in relation to the far higher idea of the dignity of humans in their Godward destiny are in perfect harmony with his Religion of Love, the mutual concern and dialogue of human and Divine.

Though gazelle-women (11–12) here may allegorize worldly distraction, as Horten suggests, and their grazing-gardens may be the lure of the merely speculative sciences, as opposed to mystic vision, my own inclination is rather to link the vision-cluster of women, gazelles, and garden to the pre-eminence of Tasting in our recommended ascent to ever fuller knowledge based on experience, on the vital reality of the perceptual world as God made it, awaking love in the several stages, all valuable, of its pleasurable progression in the rich imaginings of our hearts. Tasting, we saw above, relates to the constantly alert receptive action recommended to us by contemplating the mind of God, Who, ever about some new task, has set the model of nano-second alterations of awareness. Plato, envisioning an imaginal-philosophic Ladder of Love in the *Symposion*, understood this well, and (as noted above) it is Plato, alone among philosophers, who for Ibn Arabi embodies the ability to taste of all the realms of Being. The grazing gazelles in the verses about women (11–12) recur in verse 13 when the poet declares that his heart is glad to be a grazing place for the amiable creatures. Verses 11–12 may well deserve a place of honor next to the Song of Solomon, to which, as we remarked (following Corbin), the entire Qur'an may aptly be compared. For Ibn Arabi, Islam may be deemed the Religion of Love, for in the Qur'an God tells the Prophet: "Say (O Muhammad, to mankind): If ye love Allah, follow me: Allah will love you. . . ." (3:31). God so loved Muhammad that He accepted him as Beloved or "Friend" (*MT* 12).

After verses 13–15, the imaginative heart of the poet's Religion of Love, it is fitting that the poet should conclude with a verse in honor of women who have emblemized, for poets of the Islamic world, the ardor that can intimate, initially at the sensory level, the delights that, when tasted, guide us upward in spirit. Laila, for example, is the heroine of a Romeo-and-Juliet story of star-crossed lovers, a legend much loved in Arabia and Persia. Members of rival clans, Laila and her suitor, called Mejnun (meaning "possessed" or "be-jinned"), were separated by their elders, who exiled the young man into the desert, where he endlessly wrote the name of his loved one in the sand. Goethe, incidentally, who wrote "You in a thousand forms yourself may hide" in a spirit recalling the love religion of Ibn Arabi (*WED* 121, poem 193, "In Tausend Formen. . ."), also identified strongly with Mejnun in his love for Laila (see *WED* 59, poem 79: "'Mejnun' means—I cannot claim / That it *really* meant 'insane'. . .").

In the second Ibn Arabi poem, "Vision of the Divine Being," the meeting depicted by the questing soul is another rite in the Religion of Love: it is a love encounter, a rendezvous. Horten writes, "The rendezvous is either (Ibn Arabi seems to find possible more than one interpretation of his poem) the waystation of belief (of the pilgrim) or the contract that God establishes with the soul. . ." (*MT* 13). The pilgrim's camels are urged to play, gazelle-like, on the grazing meadow. "Play," says Ibn Arabi, "betokens the changing conditions in which the mystic is placed when following the Divine Names, one after another. The gazelles and maidens represent the abstract and deep-rooted [spiritual] sciences of unification with God" (*MT* 14). Ever-altering awareness, the motion-component of Ibn Arabi's epiphanic pattern, is playful, experimental, adventurous. "The meadow," he adds, "is the presence of God bound up with the Holy Names contained in Him" (*MT* 14). Wind-breath and meadow alike are Godly attributes that emblemize the beauty of His world; lightning and thunder represent, in turn, intuitive contemplation of God and the startling noumenon of conversation with Him.

1 ~ GOD THE ALL-IMAGINER

Ibn Arabi adds: "Raindrops (no streaming rain) are the manifold individual types of awarenesses of God"—again we have the epiphanic theme, the spiritual and experiential ideal, of perpetually varying states of awareness. Each raindrop is a uniquely enjoyable, distinct moment of perception. A playful attitude is intrinsic to our pilgrimage, and entertainments are among our valued waystations.

The mystic wine of love is our pilgrim-solace. Notes Ibn Arabi, "This wine comes and flows forth from the presence of God, which establishes its dwelling in the soul of the mystic and indeed in the time of its growth." Adds Horten, "...God begins to live in the heart of the mystic when the latter is only a novice, a beginner on the road to spiritual life" (*MT* 15). And who are the fair maidens? For Ibn Arabi and Horten (*MT* 15–16), they are "the Divine Names (and thus: manifestations of God's inner Being): from the spice box we enjoy the mystical station of speech and of the expression of thought (colloquy of the soul with God), and the modest virgins represent the station of modesty, i.e., of contemplation (of God)."

The third poem, "Apotheosis of the Human," depicts the fruitful hardships of the ascetic and the need for a patient response, like that of the camels, unfailingly devoted in their uncomplaining aid. The temple is the mystic heart, the mortifying hardships are the needed renouncings. Interpreting the conclusion in verse 7, and with it the whole poem, Ibn Arabi says, "I professed to love God, yet complained of being tired and sleepy. But the camels, who are my acts and thoughts which I lead and control, utter no complaint" (*MT* 17). When, in poem 33 above, we heard Ibn Arabi describe reason, habit, and imagination, it seemed that these three might be ascending waystations, and here they are exactly that. Speculative intellect is less central to growth than experiential perception and spiritual tasting. Habit is higher if we daily accustom ourselves to thought and action that befit the pilgrim. And thus may we hope to reach, with grace, the goal of our Imagination, which is to be blent with the One Who is the All-Imaginer.

(8) The Beauty of Love in Calligraphy

We have learned from Ibn Arabi that the world we live in arose from the sigh of God, a Lover who wanted to be loved. In the painting he has kindly allowed me to present on the cover of this book, calligrapher Shahid Alam quotes a saying of Ibn Arabi that he translates, "Love is my religion and my faith" (for two other versions of this, see "Boundless Love," I. 5, xliv and "Equal Worth of All Religions," verse 15, 137). Shahid further explains the implications of the calligraphic painting, where he has not only cited but emblemized that central guiding principle stated by the greatest theosopher of Sufism:

> The Sun as source of Love. In a desert landscape two green oases are born. The script is in white and brown: "Love is my religion and my faith" is written twice, above and below.

In the essay "Art Bridges," appended to this volume, Shahid further notes the observation ascribed to the Prophet, "God is beautiful and He loves beauty." In the poem below, taking my cue from a valuable statement by Johan Huizinga offered as epigraph, I suggest that a helpful definition of the Divine beauty might be the well-known summary afforded by St. Thomas Aquinas (ca. 1225–1274), a thinker who flourished a few decades after Ibn Arabi (1165–1220), and who is comparable to him in spiritual stature. St. Thomas, writing in Latin, offers three conceptual keys to beauty. These are *integritas, consonantia,* and *claritas*—completeness, harmony, and brightness. I contemplate the three keys in a poem:

On The Beauty of God in His Script

"Allah is beautiful and He loves beauty."
—Hadith Sahīh Muslim 911

"De Pulchritudine Dei et Venustate Mundi" [On the Beauty of God and the Attractiveness of the World] —title of a book by Denis the Carthusian

"Three things, says Saint Thomas, are required for beauty: first, integrity or perfection, because what is incomplete is ugly on that account; next, true proportion or consonance; lastly, brightness, because we call beautiful whatever has a brilliant colour. Denis the Carthusian tries to apply these standards. . . . [W]e notice that nearly always when men of the Middle Ages attempt to express aesthetic enjoyment, their emotions are caused by sensations of luminous brightness or of lively movement."
—see J. Huizinga, The Waning of the Middle Ages *266–9*

That God is beautiful Islamic teaching tells:
Completeness, Plenitude of Being—that is He;
Proportion, Consonance in Him will likewise be;
We Splendor call the light where moving life upwells.

Each word Qur'anic through calligraphy excels
In mirroring that wholeness, concord, brilliancy:
For every word is an artistic unity
Where letters harmonize, combine their beauty-spells.

Bright feeling from the lively movement in the realm
Of interacting letters well may overwhelm
The reader with a verve and surge: we fly and flow

And feel a new Becoming in the Being, so
That deepened by the wisdom, speeded by the flame
Of Spirit fast advancing, we will say His name.

In applying the same criteria found in Divine beauty to works of calligraphic art which are also readable statements of Islamic themes, I use an insight that Shahid has expressed in public lectures on traditional calligraphic art based on Arabic script.

Shahid explains that in each calligraphic word the shapes of the Arabic letters are *modified so as to harmonize with each other.* I have never heard such a principle enunciated as governing any other kind of calligraphic practice. The consequence of it is that *every word is a work of art.*

Completeness, integrity, and fullness of being are manifested in every artistically shaped word. Harmony, consonance, proportion will be shown in every word, as well. And the brightness, the liveliness, of the calligraphic word is double: we receive the intelligible and imaginative meaning at the same time that we feel our spirits animated by the beauty of the forms made with the *qalam,* the bamboo writing reed.

To this I would add another striking consequence of the practice whereby every word becomes a work of art, of enjoyable and palpable beauty, namely that *every word may be viewed as an emblem of love.* The shape of each letter is lovingly, empathetically adapted to the forms of all the others, so that the desired concord guides every stroke. The unit is complete, a plenitude of being, in its embodiment of that concord. And the lively brightness of the feeling that ensues in the viewer is the crowning effect of that concord. Love is the guide to this treasurable form of art.

Shahid has made 27 full-page calligraphies of the respective names of all the prophets interviewed by Ibn Arabi in *Bezels*, the narrative of his tour of the heavenly spheres which pre-dates the celestial journey taken by Dante (ca. 1265–ca.1321) in his *Paradiso*. The calligraphic name of each heaven-dweller is always put on the page directly facing the poem (or the first poem, if there are more than one) based on the interview with him. Straight lines and curves predominate in the designs.

The *alif*, opening letter of the Arabic alphabet, is a straight vertical line. Since, as I learned from a hand therapist when recovering from carpal tunnel syndrome some years back, the most relaxed and restful position for the human hand is a fist, it may be useful to think of the rounded fist as the fetal position, so to speak, of the hand. Then, as the fist opens up and the palm and fingers straighten in a vertical line, we may say the *alif* of creative possibility is opened, as when Allah, often called in Qur'anic language the Cleaver of the Daybreak, brought light into the world as distinct from darkness with a single stroke. The darkness of the dormant or pre-creative circle awakens, uncurves, and yields to the light as it is re-formed into the straight line of making.

Parables

(1) Ibn Arabi Speaks

I am the secret of the sigh that can appease
What only can be called the sadness of the One,
The longing of the treasure that is not yet known
Until the being who'll reveal it in his form

By love-awareness will awake, an angel-sun,
To manifest the Name that Holy Breathing, warm
Amid innumerable Virtualities,
Will bring to life in Beauty seen, and Beauty shown.

A night of spirit I endured in temple-shade
Until by con-spiration, of com-passion made,
By adoration I might let the treasure be

That longing breathed, creating both itself and me.
Who sighed to be revealed is comforted when I
Alive in that desire can vanish in that sigh.

(2) Ibn Arabi Tells of Angels

Three angels came. And Abraham, their mortal host,
Provided them with nourishment. And thus will do
The human following Qur'an-advice: return
Unto *your* Lord. For any God that we may know

Is angel, radiant embodiment, at most,
Of Hidden Being. And he'll come, inviting you
To know yourself in him revealed, resurgent learn—
Through more transcendings—of the One Concealed,
    and grow

As angel-forms at every stage to you appear
Whom you have earned the right to view in what they
    will
More deeply, highly manifest. No striving ends

The messenger-succession of transcendent friends.
Let One Who's never known through finite vision-
    skill
Be welcomed in the guest. Your Name today you'll
    hear.

(3) Ibn Arabi Tells of the Face

'All things will perish,' we remember, 'but His face,'
Unending Image of the One. But objects mirror
The Shaper Who had made them: therefore all things
    die
Except the faces of those things. The Prophet saw

One youth, supreme in beauty, as the form of grace
That Angel Gabriel put on, a vision clearer
Than what his baffled friends were lent. But you
    and I
Will like the truth, surviving, that one hears in awe.

The Queen of Sheba when she viewed the polished
    floor
Of Solomonic hall, would lift, as if on shore,
Her gown, unwettened by what seemed a gleaming
    sea.

The palace and the hall are gone. The metaphor
Of water will remain, and still must mean to me:
The hue of your container will your spirit be.

(4) Ibn Arabi Tells of Families

The subtle body-forms of interworlding Cloud
Engender holy families that blend the Names.
While Adam God-like fathered Eve, a complement
Appeared when Mary, like Sophia, mothered Christ.

As Holy Wisdom and the Lord we are allowed
To call a Queen and King, the gladsome poet claims
That Eve and Jesus were the loving siblings lent
To vision twinned with lauding word, imparadised.

When Fátima of Córdoba my mother met,
She said, 'O light! Behold my son, your father, too.'
The Prophet's daughter, 'mother of her father' named,

As Fátima the Radiant would be acclaimed.
So Khidr, Khádir, Green One, brother, father, let
Me have his prophet-mantle, that the spirits view.

(5) Ibn Arabi Tells of Light and Wind

One who Unveiling underwent was terrifed—
Returned and trembled, shaken. So I scolded him:
'You feared the quenching of what lordliness you
    had.'
Let one who wants to be illumined rather come

Without a glory-torch of magnifying pride—
At most a wick unlit or twig asmolder, dim,
So mighty wind may fan a glimmer, make it glad:
The cresset, the flambeau is quelled, but halidom

Of breath will make a tiny votive candle grow.
The heat of high resolve, well-based, will be enough.
Enflamed by this, a quiet warmth in servant-will

The waiting one, beloved of the God, may fill.
The prostrate grasses wait: wind gusty, blust'ring,
    rough,
Invigorates, not breaks them, bent, who pray below.

(6) Ibn Arabi Tells of the Horn

Imagination emblemed is in shape a horn,
Much like the final trumpet that Seraphiel
Two times will play, when all who live on earth, in
    sky,
Will faint, then rise to an accounting with their Lord.

At first the tip, the highest part of it, is born,
The point to which all rise that of the One may tell.
The widest round below is Interworld, where lie,
Upon Two Oceans' Meeting Place, things metaphored.

Here honey, milk are knowledge, wine and pearls.
    The form
Of Íslam is a dome, a pillar. The Qur'an
Is honey, butter. And religion is a cord—

The Real a light, a human being. Cold and warm,
Earth, air, fire, water—we in all of these the dawn,
The Cleaver of the Daybreak, face in joy's reward.

(7) Ibn Arabi Tells of Breath

Our Interworld, the Breath Divine's a lover-sigh
To lessen a constriction, give the Yearner ease
From pressure of the Names that, forcing forth,
    would be
Made known, for what is treasure if it stay unfound?

He breathed the lover-words that round about us lie,
He rendered visible the virtualities,
The canticle He sang let last, unfailingly,
You, His beloved, who can echo back the sound!

Mind knows, and body moves: Imagination makes
Of Milk a Knowledge metaphor. God-Constancy
By faithful hearts affirmed whenever morning breaks

We emblem in a cord. The Primal Word was 'Be.'
Replying to His Love, we heard before we saw.
He gave us breath, and takes our breath away in
    awe.

(8) Ibn Arabi Tells of Tasting

Reflection adds to tasting no sensation new—
Yet when you eat an apple, every bite you take
From every other bite may have a different taste.
You'll feel that tasting, drinking, quenching are the
    three

Degrees or waking-stages of unveiling. View
Friend, messenger, and prophet—wine with these will
    make
Three knowing-levels, though the friend may well be
    graced
With all of them. A man who tastes a calm may be,

Though hungry, yet from any agitation free
While one who's never tasted of tranquillity
Might lack the patient skill to wait, although aware

That someone will his dinner very soon prepare.
The food is brought—yet he's no calmer than the one
Who's confident that God will let the blessing come.

(9) Ibn Arabi Tells of the Names of Adam

We know that God 'taught Adam all the names.' But,
    too,
We're told He gave His Form to Adam. Thus we know
His Names, the ninety-nine, the beautiful, the Lord
Ascribed to us, and then the pre-creation Trust

That God had offered we accepted, I and you—
We had the courage other creatures lacked, the glow
Of all the ninety-nine, His mirrors, in accord
If we but lead the Life Unveiled, and so we must.

'My earth and sky embrace Me not,' He would
    declare,
'But My believing servant does embrace Me.' Naught
Is like Him, yet His Face—we find it everywhere.

Uniqueness, root divine and quarry, we are taught,
Belong to us and Him, and likeness, too. With care
He made us, part alike, yet each beyond compare.

(10) Ibn Arabi Tells of Throwing

We say, 'You threw not when you threw, but Allah
    threw'
The spear that met the mark. What may that
    scripture mean?
If you have thrown with more perfection than a man
Is wont to show, you bodied forth a Godly Name.

But treasure must be found, and Being isn't true
Unless by one imagined known, in spirit seen.
The human is the Name in action, therefore can
To be self-knowledge of the Maker-Poet claim.

'By knowing Him I give Him being.' So I wrote.
The creature is creative when he mirrors back
The passion that conceived him, out of Being's lack.

The Lord is thought, and known, and loved, and
    longed for when
The canticle is answered in the realm of men:
The heart sang, 'Be," and we have harmonized that
    note.

(11) Ibn Arabi Tells of Shared Being

Halláj had said, 'I am the Truth.' And I have heard
Some people claim that they are one with God.
   Instead,
I merely came to Him with love, Who His Qur'an
To me had chanted, Song of Songs, to win my heart.

I give Him Being with my love, for in His Word
The Hidden showed a psalming that, when it was
   read,
Would swift allure the treasure-finder, leading on
The hearer smitten, given Being by His art.

We're Solomon and Loved One each, reciprocate
Our Being-gifts. I know in Him the Name, the fate,
The aptitude He'd planned to body forth in me,

Platonic Form of what, in Him, I yet might be.
I nourish Him when I His treasure-depth can heed,
As Abraham the angels three was blest to feed.

(12) Ibn Arabi Tells of Movement

The body—Temple true. But who are worshipers?
The pray'rful one, alone, is imam, leader, when
The subtle souls of every part and organ chant
In chorus: many-hundred-fold, the service heard.

Positions three for him—erect, low bow, and then
A full prostration on the rug. The Lord confers
The favor of the same—the motions come again:
In Gabriel descending to reveal the Word,

Then rearising. God, with clouds at eventide,
Will join horizon-borders, wider Life extend.
In man erect, and in the animals that grow

In horizontal motion, plants that downward tend
For nourishment of root, three movements, too,
   abide.
The greater world we mirror, praising. Be it so.

(13) Ibn Arabi Tells of Beliefs

Beliefs are made. In turn explore each one, and learn
The circumstances where they reasonably came
To be, what need they answered. Hidden God
    transcends
The knotting any single strong belief may cause.

Be matter to receive new faith-forms. Never spurn
That manifold. To each of us the Godly Name
We clearly most embody singularly lends,
Though one be unaware, delimitation-laws.

Investigate all doctrines. Learn with care the place
Proponents came from, molding them to formulate
Their sayings. You may then support and laud each
    one

As rightful in a context of the time and space
And mode that it arose in. To the Godly state
No pilgrim solely holds the entry-benison.

(14) Ibn Arabi Tells of the Sun and Moon

Two God-revealings mind will equally amaze.
We're blinded by the sun. Indeed, enfolding veils
Of Him are seventy—of light and dark they're made:
Remove them—and the glory of the Face would burn

Creation with Divine annihilating rays.
Yet in the gentle moon-shape, too, the pilgrim hails
The Glow—or, in the brightness of the light allayed
At noon, we view the creatures and their Lord in
    turn.

Waystations on the visionary path include
The two disclosure-modes. The moon revealed to me
How large in little shows, when through the needle
    may

The camel pass. For by the eyes are we endued
With vision higher than our reason. One I see
Who'll widen heart at night to hold Eternal Day.

(15) Ibn Arabi Tells of the Chameleon

'Each day' we are informed, the Lord's 'upon some
　　task.'
Yet beings varied in awareness differently
Can live a 'day': its length is alterable. Thus
An angel day is fifty thousand years. If in

The 'twinkling of an eye' be God's command, we ask:
Need not the deed required proportionable be
In time to that request? A task-day will for us
Be every atom-moment. Wake, let work begin!

No attribute, no state remains for even two
Of all our minutes. The chameleon has grown
To feel the force of quick-as-lightning change and
　　known

More vividly than any creature what a new
Creation every moment means. In dreams alone
Can world-transforming eye-blink motion so be
　　shown.

(16) Ibn Arabi Tells of the Unique

The Sufi gnostic knows of God but cannot tell
What in the heaven-realm he will have tasted. While
Our tastings of an earthly object we compare
And, if alike, we tag them with a single word,

The Lord can not be likened. Thus the God that I'll
Perceive will not be yours. Nor ever twice befell
Unaltered view to one of His belauders. Where
Diversity of God is daily felt and heard

In spiritual tasting, knowledge deeper grows:
I more about the Real perceived each time He rose.
The changing types of faith are valid, but they're
    knots—

And tie you down. Be claylike matter: let the
    thoughts
That body forth the Names in varied form impress
Your heart, and may their holy shapes combine to
    bless.

(17) Ibn Arabi Tells of Milk

The Prophet drank in dream a cup of milk and knew
That ev'n his fingertips were sated: he explained
The nourishment was knowledge. I, one time, a
    spring
Of milk in vision entered till it reached my chest.

The withness of the Real so daily will endue
The creature. Yet the nearness that we've thus
    attained
Is one-way. Though we witness in our burgeoning
Continual disclosure, Essence hid will rest.

Imagination governs everything we know:
The world we feel is God's imagining, and so
He's nearer than our jugular. He's everywhere

We go. The milk in which I bathed from holy spring
Will never fail if only I, a servant, cling
To knowledge—ever-present in the breath of air.

(18) Ibn Arabi Tells of a Cave

When we are told to 'flee to God,' let's run away
From ignorance to knowledge, narrow to the wide—
Not leave the world. So Plato tasted every state
Of Being, and could feel the high in low, and stayed.

'Increase me in the knowledge,' we will gladly say,
'Of You and of Your manifested Names.' Abide
In trying. Though your pain and poverty be great—
By independence, nondistraction, gains are made.

When only narrowness the Prophet viewed in men
The cave he fled to for awhile would shape again
The face of God he saw within each one. The cave

Renewed the God-in-Worldliness that aids the brave.
A physical retreat you won't indeed require:
Flee readily to inner depth, revived desire.

(19) Ibn Arabi Tells of Iron and Ruby

When idle talk is heard by friends of God they go
Without distraction past, and prove nobility.
'I am Alláh' and 'Glory give to me' appear
Among the idle thoughts of one who yet remains

A well-intentioned man, Abú Yazíd. We know
A Higher Fullness when the Names Divine that we,
In trying to assume their features, feel endear
The pilgrim by the distance each of them retains.

I'm just the iron weight—to counter it is weighed
A bright, unequaled Ruby. Quantity I bring,
But not the Being. Radiant, transparent, He.

A self-revealing knowledge cannot be assayed
If yet we taste a foreign lordship-flavoring.
The noble will the Ruler serve with courtesy.

(20) Ibn Arabi Tells of Boredom

Self-boredom gains a victim when you, blind, forget
That though your essence may remain, contingent
    traits—
Each thought and impulse, mood and feeling—
    momently
Can alter. In the living form of God you're made.

A stable self-disclosure, prison-trap, may let
A veil, that hides divinity and life abates,
Prevent you from progressing. Waken, then, and see
God, human, every minute changed when faith-
    portrayed.

To yearn for the beloved more of bliss can give
Than limitless companionship. In Eden, too,
Continual are parting, re-encounter. You

No paradise would feel, did not the Lord renew
The lessening and re-inciting. Souls that live
Each moment will a novel God-disclosure view.

(21) Ibn Arabi Tells of Modesty

As God is beautiful, loves beauty, and by Names
Which are most perfect in their beauty may be
    known,
So too, a character that's beautiful will be
The best of all the parts of faith and on the Day

Of Judgment will be duly weighed. The Prophet
    claims
That all religions moral characters have shown—
The one that's chief in Islam being Modesty.
To realize the Names of beauty best, we may

Attention focus on the Great Surrender, on
The transformation of the heaven by the dawn
And pray with Abraham the door be opened wide

Whereby the Lord our heart may enter and abide.
They're merely shadows dancing on a darkened wall
On whom the rushing flood of Light has yet to fall.

(22) Ibn Arabi Tells of the Root

Prostration means that to the Root we homage pay:
It's of the nature of a root to be unseen.
A shade protected from annihilating sun,
The shadow thus will bow to what remains unviewed.

The heart, though fluctuant by nature, yet will stay
Forever prostrate, for the homage here will mean
A fealty owed to Names that, hid from everyone,
Have caused the fluctuations that to God allude.

The shadows prostrate bow to light they cannot see,
The reeds will prostrate bend to wind they only feel:
The shadow, reed, and heart would never come to be,

Nor would their light and wind and stir, without the Real.
No state more noble than prostration can we know,
For straightway to the root of Being will it go.

(23) Ibn Arabi Tells of the Waystations

The stations on the way are Names you enter when
You feel prepared. If Patience be the Godly place
You've chosen, every moment more will you acquire
Of changing wisdom: so will Patience be revealed.

The servant, learner, will be pleased each time again
He gets to know a virtue, and the Master grace
And favor gains: a holy Name, by shared desire,
Is realized, admired, and loved, and unconcealed.

And if the pupil, vassal, gladly would remain
Far longer, then the station an abode will be:
The virtue-Name, unchanged, will alter as the new

Perfections of the chosen quality you gain
That alter by the moment. Many faces He
Displays in the created world, so here to you.

(24) Ibn Arabi Tells of the Cup

Junayd said, Water will the cup's own color take—
The Essence of the Real can not be named or known.
It has to be made manifest. I gladly drink
What my preparédness had made me thirsty for.

My character and nature and the use I make
Of what has happened, what I'm given, how I've
    grown
Will shape the cup that holds what I suppose I
    think—
Yet water into endless vessel-kinds He'll pour.

Manát, al-Lát, and al-Uzzáh, the females three
Who each had been considered, once, a deity
Were thus a triple apparition of the Real.

The Face of God is everywhere, but He has made
All things in measure, in the hues of Names arrayed.
From colored cup we drink what we in spirit feel.

(25) Ibn Arabi Tells of the Knot

Beliefs are knots—can tie you up, or down. And yet
The intricacy of a knot we may admire,
The beauty of its making laud. The Sufi tries
Each one, for all are of the Real. Our minds are wide

And may all things include, save Hidden Being. Let
Us tie the knots and learn their making. 'Twill
    require
Undoing each before we try the next: the eyes
All beauties cannot view together. We'll abide

With each belief, assume it, feel it, live it, and
The range of emblems value that with bounteous
    hand
The Real, the Hidden Being glad will grant—but,
    still,

Remain unbound, unlimited by any. We
Can nothing but belief that is conditioned see:
The tying and unbinding many lives would fill.

(26) Ibn Arabi Tells of Imagination

Whoever apprehends a thing with outward sense
Or inner, will imagine. Reason, too, may be
Required to think of what has not yet been, and
   then—
Imagination, vital hidden strength, will act.

The human heart and mind are changeably intense,
And thus with revelations of the Names agree—
Chameleon-colored, mind and heart, in mortal men.
All's pictured but the Essence—hidden, single fact.

Your face will not be greatly altered day by day:
The micro-changes in each atom are unseen.
Within, what fluctuation! Vim of whimsied mood!

But in the world to come, your inner state will stay
More fixed, intent upon the One, Supreme, Serene—
Yet—outwardly—each moment you will be renewed.

(27) Ibn Arabi Tells of the Heart

The heart, by nature ever changing, fluctuates:
When held between the Lord's two fingers, it will
    turn
To that side or to this—to pound excited, or
Be calm, observing what might bale or bliss appear.

Embracing, glad, it undelimited awaits
With every moment new unfolding: it will learn
With understanding vast, imaginal—adore,
Upwelling in a welcoming, its Kaaba clear.

Within the stable nature of our God will be
A varicolored life in high variety.
Yet will the Turner of the Heart be merciful:

Apparent wrath must toward the Lord's compassion
    pull.
For wisely every failing He'll in time forgive—
And in the mercy of that Heart my heart will live.

(28) Ibn Arabi Tells of Faith

When Satan, in the form beguiling of a man
Attractive, old, and handsome, tried to make the
    Christ
Obey his order, feed his pride, he said, 'Declare:
There is no god but God.' 'I will, but not because

I'm ordered. There's no god but God.' And so we can,
Observing, learning, heeding, never be enticed
To bend, in faith, to man's command. No tyrant-dare
Avails. We've 'no compulsion in religion.' Pause,

Recall, take heart: when Adam to the offered Trust
Of God replied acceptingly, his word conveyed
To humankind a heritage, and now we must

Be stewards of the earth, by first agreement made
Attentive to that covenant, a primal law
To guide our nature, manifest in humble awe.

(29) Ibn Arabi Tells of Poverty

The Prophet told of waiting by the Garden gate,
The entrants mainly poor. The rich 'imprisoned'
    were—
For these, who grasp the Real in what a man might
    own,
Are vainly circumspect and burdened down with
    care.

One coin outweighs a thousand, we may calculate,
If it be spent for God. The rich man who'd confer
A thousand in a gift, great wealth might leave alone
In coffer, counted, wasted. Feel the empty air—

'No-thing'—how large, how undelimited!—where we
Are destitute of everything but God—Who told
The Prophet, 'Nothing of command belongs to you.'

Receiver of the changing Revelation be:
They're trapped who would command what shall be
    bought and sold.
The Prophet-poor this limitation will undo.

(30) Ibn Arabi Tells of the Straight Path

The path of God is straight, and all to Him return.
'Each crawling thing,' indeed, He'll 'by the forelock'
   take,
Directing it aright. All paths may not the same
Felicity exhibit—straight, though, are they all.

He's with you, like the treasuries of things, we learn.
The whispering, the witnessing that God will make
He will to suit your level of attainment frame
Replying to the Name you mirror, know, and call.

As universal matter every form assumes,
The comprehending Withness of the Lord will mean
He brings together, infinitely, all the Names.

How strange to know the straightness all the varied
   claims
To aptitude and truth will bring to light. Serene,
He animal, plant, human movement each illumes.

(31) Ibn Arabi Tells of Time

God is a nightless and a never-ending Day.
In telling Moses, 'Be attentive to the days
Of God,' He meant the means whereby each Name
    Divine,
A quality or attribute, is manifest.

Such days are of the Soul and in a wonder-way
Will interpenetrate, commingle—each with rays
That we may view and know, but, too, their nights
    confine
Our sight of things yet unrevealed. And both are
    best.

Prophetic narrative will tell you: Time's a Name
Of Him, and in that Time we flourish on a tree.
He is the root, and we the fruit and boughs—yet, too,

The tree of world-existence equally might claim
To be pervaded with the brave command: to Be.
A branch, a fruit—a Name of Him, it, me, and you.

(32) Ibn Arabi Tells of Prayer

'The giving of your Lord' can't be 'walled up,'
    withheld.
But maybe you are soothed by sun at height of noon
While someone different-natured overheated feels:
A wind puts out a candle, or will fan a blaze.

The present and your preparation-level meld:
Our varied receptivity to us a boon,
A blessing, or a thing of less effect reveals.
You may have reached fit asking-level, yet have days

Or years to go before the getting-level's fit
For what you wanted to be best for you. We knit
A garment not yet wearable who pray too fast.

And 'man is made of haste.' For benefit to last,
I'd ask, in prayer, for preparédness to be
My gift—to be enriched by receptivity.

(33) Ibn Arabi Tells of Three Talismans

Three talismans reveal their strong validity.
The Reason vigor lends to demonstrate we know
Of nothing whatsoever but through God. Alas,
Too many turn it upside down and proudly say,

'You nothing know of God, O Reason, but through
    me.'
Another talisman, our habits, pow'r may show
To rule. Imaginings, third talisman, will pass
To view the very being of the world when they

Reveal the Lord as Similar. Contingency,
The Possible, reside within the Real. When we
Have understood that grounded root, we rise, and
    He,

Without a substrate, will His own identity
Unfold, but in a way unique, ineffably,
To each receiver, who will view Him differently.

(34) Ibn Arabi Tells of Master and Sons

There's conflict in your life among the varied claims
Upon your thought, awareness, action. Many are
The Names of God. If one will call to you, perhaps
You'll turn away, preferring still the one that called

You earlier. Its term is over. No one blames
Your tension while you try to comprehend the far
Extending implication of the change that taps
Potential to prevent your growth from being stalled.

If you would work for life and Lord, recall that He's
The Master, and the Names of Him, the attributes,
Are many sons, with varied personalities.

The servant all of them not equally can please—
Adapt yourself, be mindful of the future fruits
The newer call may bring—reply to it with ease.

(35) Ibn Arabi Tells of Courtesy

The courteous will grant to everything its due—
To friend and guest and spouse, to body, soul, and
 eye.
Fulfilling Trust agreed upon in primal days,
He'll gather all the best to virtue's banquet hall.

Religion formed a code of courtesy for you:
The Prophet courtesy was taught by Him on high
And called it 'beautiful.' That beauty may we praise
In one who things of beauty brings together. Call

Him master of that virtue who the noble traits
Of character can grasp and tries to make the heart
A locus where they congregate, for he has learned

To tell the high from lower qualities and states,
And hallowed Names will value where the cosmic art
Had primal cause, and honor in the world has
 earned.

(36) Ibn Arabi Tells of Struggle

God told the Prophet that the spear which he had
    thrown
With miracle-result had not by him been cast
But rather by the Lord Himself. A question-'test'
We have when we inquire: was God my helper here?

God loves a struggler more than him who'll sit alone
At home and never move. Along with standing fast
In will to action, though, we give the Lord our best
Who know that freedom baffles, yet who have no fear.

With novel Name He may tomorrow call on you,
And myriad aiding angels may He send—or not.
They struggle well within the Lord who've taken
    thought

Regarding how their acts awake. They struggle
    'through'
The One, and not against Him, who in faithful ways
The query-test can welcome, and His Glory praise.

(37) Ibn Arabi Tells of the Polished Surface

Upon a polished, gleaming surface when we view
A mirrored thing, we look with pleasure, but will not
Direct our thinking to the surface, or the eye's
Alertness, and the mind and heart, are turned aside

From what we looked at—empathy is lessened, too.
So from the locus of disclosure will our thought
Be turned away, the Lord unseen. And yet the wise
Recall: the thing is light, and will in light abide.

The Real, the Lord revealed, is light, and in the light
We see it—light, in light enfolded, speedily
Re-meets the cause from which it came. The one
    who'll see

The object that he made is no one else than He.
In radiance from Him alone we're granted sight,
And 'mid the things made visible is yet more light.

(38) Ibn Arabi Tells of the King's Command

An Inrush may imperil when the force outweighs
A mind that undergoes a visit, and goes mad.
But if one's fortitude be great, the heart will change
In ways controllable—peculiar, though, to see.

Let's say you're talking to a friend, and he displays
A mood you vaguely feel and can't explain, a glad
Distraction, partly mastered. Then he may arrange
A pat reply—but wavering, evasively.

He's thinking of the messenger who had
    approached—
Invisible, delivering a king's command.
Imagination can this Inrush understand

Though you may have no clue he's inwardly been
    coached
Save for a dulling gaze and failure to respond
And stubborn concentration on a hint beyond.

(39) Ibn Arabi Tells of the Form in the Mirror

The world is Undelimited Imagination—
For all's imagined but the Essence of the Lord
Whose nature none can know. Thus every creature made
Is nonexistent, and exists—and neither one.

Imaginings no affirmation or negation
Depicts. They're neither known nor *un*known, but accord
With ontologic indistinction. They are shade
And light, and both and neither. Darkness? Or a sun?

You're looking in a mirror, see your form, and know
You've seen your form, and know your form's not in the mirror,
Nor does it float between the mirror and your eye.

'I saw my form, I didn't see my form.' You show
It won't get disambiguated. Can't be clearer:
You neither told the truth, nor did you tell a lie.

(40) Ibn Arabi Tells of the Two Eyes

Though by the Lord viceregal power we're assigned
To govern things within the world, we need them
    more
Than they need us. I care must therefore take to be
Their steward, viewing Him in each, a witness true

Of God on things' behalf, that He may be divined
In love and in awareness of the cosmos. Pour
Your thanks from out an overflowing soul, for we
Are poor toward the world. I've learned what we
    must do:

Things trusting in our human stewardship I view
With two-eyed vision, as He meant. I first adore
The unknown Being they betoken, ready for

The manifesting in the objects that on me
Depend, to whom they'll show their similarity
To God. My second eye will metaphors renew.

(41) Ibn Arabi Tells of Recompense

Existence you are granted, but you only give
Yourself reward in being able to accept:
Waystation reached, Form entered, mirrored, and
    attained
Determines openness to what the Real bestows.

The recompense whereby you deeply feel you live
Will be your self-disclosure in the mirror kept
Within the Name that called, that you in turn have
    gained:
Diverse the Name-awakening the Perfect knows.

A dawning is a resurrecting: it can be
Reward that, newly named, made life more truly
    known—
So novel the unfolding every moment shown,

Imagination of a possibility
Will be a seed of light new-sown, a ray immense:
You clove the daybreak and invoked a recompense.

(42) Ibn Arabi Tells of the Lover's Names

The thrall beloved of the Lord on His effects
Within the heart will look, and pray the Name
    beheld.
The loved one called, 'Creator!' 'Here I am' is heard;
'O All-Provider!' 'Here I am.' 'O Strong!' 'To you

I answer.' Doubly loving bond of these directs
The Lover- and beloved-longing, them to meld
In single will, with Being shared in urgent word.
The faces of our great Divinity are two:

The one at the Creation gazes, which it made
And where the Deity's made radiant—the next
Directed to the Hidden, not by humans known.

Within the cosmos, with the Light Divine displayed,
Abides each Name Most Beautiful in daybreak-text—
By loved one to be cried in rapt, devoted moan.

(43) Ibn Arabi Tells of Treasuries

'There is no thing whose treasuries are not with
 Us'—
Potential infinite through generative Being.
In darkened state of pre-existent potency
Things thinkable are veiled from self-awareness yet,

But when commanded to exist, they, clamorous,
Reply: 'We want to aid You, taste the Real and,
 seeing
That help to every heart is added favor, we
Will feel the present, honored, as a coronet.

We're each a place of an embodiment, can see
That He's, through each, the only viewer—Treasury
Of start, and aim, and alteration, all agreeing.

We're realized in measure, and in time and space:
God's great Creation-throne was 'on the water'—
 fleeing,
Returning: worlds are yet re-yearning for His grace.

(44) Ibn Arabi Tells of Darkness Visible

Command and word are of the spirit: they are Light,
The making-means whereby the Lord in Nature acts.
She, too, between the high Creator and the dust
Of matter prime, unformed, in mixed and middle
   state

A ray will show. If, dull in mood, you feel the night
A mere non-being, empty, re-imagine facts:
We view it! And if we behold it, then it must
Illumine. Having twofold Being, 'twill relate

As dark to light-imbuing Spirit, true, and yet
Show bright compared to nothingness or total void:
'Tis intermediary, lightened, blent, allóyed.

Imagine space and time and sky-capacity:
Not vacuous but vast are these revealed to be—
They're matrices that urge the World-Soul to beget.

(45) Ibn Arabi Tells of the Council

In poverty of yearning, uncreated things
Had craved to overcome their narrow shadow-state
Of possibility and, to the Names Divine,
Cried, 'Make us actual, and we'll repay the debt:

You'll be revealed by deed, feel strength-awakenings.'
'You're right,' the Names replied. They waited for the
    great
Name Powerful, who said, 'I'm not the first in line:
I help Desiring. Go—from him more aid you'll get.'

Desiring countered, 'Knowing knows far more than I.'
The latter gathered all the Names in Council. Then
The Name of Lordly Presence sent them forth again

And, through the Spokesman with the Name of
    Speaker, showed
The links among the Names to unmade things on
    high.
And then—the first created thing in daybreak
    glowed!

(46) Ibn Arabi Tells of the Divine Marriage

A nonexistent, not yet manifested thing
Attention welcomes of a deep-desiring love
From Being, the Creating One, the Real, and this
Will let the entity so favored be His wife.

Each Name Most Beautiful, whom God is gladdening,
Will revel in the holy wedding feast above
With newborn entity to share the waking-bliss,
For Names thereby attain a fresh creative life.

The God-engendered marriage will a fated course
Continue faithfully. No ending or divorce
The contract marital may ever nullify.

The child, existent entity, with Being graced,
Can daily, nightly, the delight entreated taste
Resulting from the love descending from on high.

(47) Ibn Arabi Tells of the Lines of Light

Celestial Earth by forecourt, or an esplanade,
Is opened out to Paradise: the other side
Extends to where we live. If at the moon or sun
Or at a lamp you look with half-shut eyes, you'll view

A network of divided lines of light, enrayed
And veiled in part by lashes. When you've slowly
    tried
To open eyelids, lines withdraw, and into one
Will gather, lamp or sun or moon composed anew.

The widened lines of light are like the forms illumed
That bodies dreaming or awaked will have assumed
In sleep, and after death, to visit Paradise,

Or like the form a spirit took when it arrived
To favor one who had the pow'r of sight revived.
The subtle shape will fade, and yet the mind entice.

(48) Ibn Arabi Tells of Even and Odd

When the Qur'an says, "By the even and the odd,"
In pairs we comprehend the Similarity
Of Him to creatures: for the Lord a metaphor,
A likeness, granted of the Highest, we become.

The even, the comparing, does He love. But God,
In high Essential Being manifest can't be.
As we are patterned on His form, we bear a core
Of likeness to each other, yet our halidom

Includes an essence unrepeatable. The Names
Of Deity are ninety-nine. The odd acclaims
The Unaccountable, supreme, Transcending One

Who is at once the shining and the blinding Sun.
Symmetric body's even-signed, each half a twin—
Five-fingered writing hand reveals the odd within.

(49) Ibn Arabi Tells of the Singular Manifold

When God first-person plural pronoun-form
    employed
In telling of His act or plan, do not suppose
That He intended in a high and regal style
A word to offer, that we might more humbly hear.

Who's nearer than our blood? And whose the light
    enjoyed,
The withness that as our companion-Sun arose
When first our wish to be made real was granted?
    While
The 'I' is God, the 'We' as well are with you here.

The holy Names of Him, the forms and functions
    made,
My ear that heard Him speak, your eye that light
    and shade
And godly veil and curtain viewed, are means
    whereby

He'll see and hear through them and us, with ear
    and eye
That are His own indeed, that He their Being lent,
An entryway to Him, by Him, the Treasure, sent.

(50) Ibn Arabi Tells of the Two Bows' Length

'Two bows' length' was the Prophet from his God, 'or
    nearer'—
Each tautened bow an arc, two circle-halves aligned.
The parts are perfect spheric Being when combined:
Muhammad was the line of separation. Clearer

The meaning here becomes, the loving lesson dearer:
Muhammad rose no more than God His head
    inclined.
The human was the line that arcs in halves confined,
A line imagined as dividing. Let the hearer

Waystation mutual now learn of, when the two
Imagined sundered arcs are joined so we can view
One sphere of Being that is human and Divine.

Let this of 'nearer' union ever be the sign:
The line is gone—there is no up or down—descend
And rise are one, and Jonah is Muhammad's friend.

(51) Ibn Arabi Tells of Patience

Who to an ugly act replies with lovely deed
Will get a wage that God the Lover joys to pay,
But misery can be a self-inflicted veil
That of your very self may hide the veiling state.

Withdraw from all contention. Yet you still are free
To lay your pain before the Lord and wailing say,
'As Job complained, so too would I.' And He will hail
Your grief: 'The caring patience you will need is
    great,

Yet only this can turn the seeming foe to friend,
Who'll be as if a brother—struggle at an end.'
Recording angels will a patient heart-love show

When seeing you've a sin committed here below:
Six hours they will delay before it's written down—
If in that time you ask for pardon, 'tis your crown.

Bezels, or Gem Settings

*with Calligraphies of the Prophets' Names
by Shahid Alam*

(52) Ibn Arabi Tells of Adam

A prophet is a bezel or a jewel setting,
The talismanic Word of him a holy seal
Protecting heaven-treasure. You the Lord shall know,
Said Adam, insofar as you by effort gain

The virtue that will let you picture your begetting
By Him, the Manifest, Imaginer, the Real.
Unknown in deepest Being, yet to you He'll show
His image in a way your nature may contain.

When Satan wouldn't bow to Adam, man of clay—
Too proud, the fiery jinn—he failed to comprehend
That when we mirror God, polarities are gone:

The high and low their being share in woken ray:
Of mud and water is the Daybreak Lord a friend,
As of the prostrate, pray'rful green we walk upon.

(53) Ibn Arabi Tells of Seth

Our second prophet, Seth, knows well the art of
    pray'r.
One feels the limit, for your essence cannot be
Denied or overburdened by a favor granted:
Divine determination is pre-measurement.

We're made of haste, we ask too fast or badly. Fair
And numberless, however, are the Names that we
Will come to know by grace accorded, never
    scanted—
As for example the Forgiver, Who'll have lent

A pardon for an error—ev'n anticipate
A peril-area: He'll guide your heart away.
Bestower, Powerful, Encompassing will change

The gifts—they strangely will be changing every day
As do the manifested forms of God the Great
In Names that varied revelation-rays arrange.

(54) Ibn Arabi Tells of Noah

Two ways to view the One—the Hid, the Manifest—
Essential Being, by no finite creature known;
And then the Real, diversely in the world portrayed:
Awareness of them both our human heart will need.

'There is naught like to Him'—in this the loftiest,
The Nature never comprehended will be shown.
Yet in the use of 'like' an implication's made:
The drive to find a likeness, too, wise dreamers heed!

'Whoever knows himself will therefore know his
   Lord.'
In this hadíth of good Rasúl a truth we find:
Waystations lower, higher, show your God and you.

The sinners who to Noah's warning had been blind
The level had not gained that knowledge would afford
Of immanent-transcendent God in balanced view.

(55) Ibn Arabi Tells of Idris / Enoch

To Enoch, who, to heaven lifted, thus may be
The man named Idris, giv'n by God a 'lofty station,'
The theme we link is that of holiness on high,
Belonging to the Elevated One, blest Name.

Though nothing's lofty but the Essence, properly
To speak (God's Inwardness, withdrawn in
    occultation),
Yet this, the Unknown Being, manifested nigh
To me and you, in you and me, we thus acclaim

As One to Whom we 'rise' in metaphor, while He
'Descends.' He's One the First, and One Alone,
    Unique.
He's in a series, yet removed. So too are we,

Who, made upon His Form, include the Names we
    seek—
The Name Alláh as well, the Hidden and the Shown:
One's inmost nature He has kept concealed,
    unknown.

(56) Ibn Arabi Tells of Abraham

The wisdom Abraham the Friend of God had brought
Resolved the problem of our freedom and our fate.
The key is mutual pervading: keep in mind
That God would be no Maker, did no World arise.

Unique among the creatures, we, in guided thought,
Become aware of this. Then know that God, though
    Great,
May not apart from Cosmos rightly be defined:
Twin mirrors, lauding, worshiping, are World and
    Skies.

We're eyes wherewith our God upon Himself will
    gaze—
Our lives determined, yes, but by the One with
    Whom
We share the deepest and the dearest Being. We,

Regarded as repliers to Divinity
By microcosmic yet reflected God, our days
Are free to shape as we Deific Light assume.

(57) Ibn Arabi Tells of Isaac

How can a ram be thought a proper ransom-fee?
A man may in his deep essential heart contain
The gnostic-known essential Being of the Lord!—
And shall a ram be claimed a payment-substitute?

When Abram dreamed he offered up his son, did he,
While dreaming, see the truth? What image did he
    gain?
A ram, *in Isaac's form!*—that Satan, with his hoard
Of lies had made appear. A simple truth, at root,

Had Abraham declared: he knew what he had
    viewed—
Imagination hadn't granted him the Real,
The later-given meaning: Let him slay a ram.

Essential heart that holds the heart of God must feel
A finite overpowered mind the great I AM
Can't wholly grasp—'twill our imaginings elude.

(58) Ibn Arabi Tells of Ishmael

'True to his promise' prophet Ishmael is called
In Scripture, clearly proving pleasing to his Lord.
'Tis helpful to remember: every human soul
Created will be counted favored, in His view—

The Workman loves the work. But who can be
    enthralled
When some men might appear to merit small
    reward?
The Names of God are many, manifold the goal,
The road, the rate of progress in the deeds we do.

A human heart may please the Name that it will
    know,
And not another Name. And who knows all the
    Names?
The Ninety-nine are groups, infinities in each.

Yet more: His Mercy will outweigh His Wrath. And so
We all return to Him, Whose Love will weigh our
    claims:
You'll find yourself at last, and Paradise will reach.

(59) Ibn Arabi Tells of Jacob

The one religion-gift that to their sons professed
Both Abraham and Jacob, was the wish Divine.
Yet God desired diverse and deeply searching
    thought
In every nation. When monastic life arose

Among the Christians, He, though—let it be
    confesssed—
The rule is not within Qur'anic law, a sign
Of will to find the Higher called it, therefore taught
Approval's due to what the well-intending chose.

The Messengers of Him are like our doctors: they
Will love the written *Wish* and, equally, the *Will*
Make bloom within your latent nature by His Names.

He's Being. Pleasure, pain are His. Who Him
    acclaims
May do it strangely, you may think, and yet fulfil
The calling of a latent nature's dawning day.

(60) Ibn Arabi Tells of Joseph

He saw eleven stars and moon and sun, who bowed
Before him. When arisen from that symbol-dream,
In later years indeed he found it coming true.
But was he not still dreaming, even while 'awake'?

The world that we inhabit God has dreamed, allowed
To be in His Imagination. We may seem
Awake but are His dream in micro-version. You
Are governed by the Names: they, when appearing,
   take

Their varied forms while being manifested by
The world supernal of Divine Imagining.
With Essence ever hidden, God imagines all

That you regard as other than yourself. Recall
What vast Imagination lives in every thing—
Breathe deep, and dream, and feel the depth of what
   is High.

(61) Ibn Arabi Tells of Hūd

'No walking being lives but by the forelock God
Will draw it. Straight the path whereon my Lord will
    be.'
So even those who, 'mid the wind-curved sandhills
    warned
By Hūd, were swept away a Mercy pure will know.

The face of God is everywhere. A deity
Of mere belief is one of limit. Even, odd—
The whole, the part is He. No doctrine need be
    scorned,
No single creed the total truth of Him will show.

We all are turned to God, Whose wrath is quelled, we
    learn,
By Mercy. Facing toward the East we worship—yet
He everywhere a morning Radiance will beget.

Receive what every teaching may of worth affirm:
A soul required to wait for Paradise will find
What hidden hope, delight, and comfort He assigned.

(62) Ibn Arabi Tells of Ṣāliḥ

Three days of mercy that the Lord, when
    Ṣāliḥ asked,
Had granted to his people may Triplicity
Of action introduce to you—above, below—
The one and many doubly thus to be combined.

The Essence: here we think of God alone. He's tasked
By Will, desire that many things may come to be.
And then the Word is said, and *Be* is heard. And so
In manifold of worlds the Maker-strength we find.

With Essence, Will, and Word we to our God reply:
Our pre-creation natures wait, till One on high
Prepare to speak the Word that we already 'hear'

In receptivity to Him. We then conform,
Compliant to command, and in the world are born
Who shared His Will that we should Be, and held it
    dear.

(63) Ibn Arabi Tells of Shu'aib

Shu'aib, whose name-root means 'diverge' or 'ramify,'
Will intimate the multiplicity and bounds
Of each belief. Our latent natures preordain
A gift and limit to our grasp, and when with heart

Alert and turned in earnest love to One on high
We seek to comprehend, the echo then resounds
Of all that longing. Even when the gnostic gains
A notion of the Hidden Essence, 'twill impart

No abrogation of his creature-limit. Those
Who think the Hidden will imagine Him as they
Were made to do by latent nature, and will say,

'Until I shall return to heaven whence I rose,
Within my bound I'll serve—I'm called upon to see
New holy things revealed that alter momently.'

(64) Ibn Arabi Tells of Lot

When Lot complained he lacked the firm support to
    win
The hearts of lower-minded folk to higher claims,
He raised a problem that will gain great interest here:
Our need for knowledge and our servanthood
    compete.

The concentrated and the focused will that in
The world can have effect to further worthy aims
May somewhat weakened be by reasonable fear
That lack of understanding may our effort greet:

The limitation of a latent nature may
The hearer foreordain to turn his face away.
The face of God is everywhere: he this will learn

But meanwhile might the word of Mercy madly
    spurn.
Is gnostic calm enough when I am called to aid?
By unfamiliar Name a summons may be made.

(65) Ibn Arabi Tells of 'Uzair / Ezra

If God rebuked 'Uzair for overeager zeal
To learn of Destiny, a bit of careful thought
Might make the prophet calmer, for whatever we
Can know of what is meant for us, we partly make.

Decree is what we call the way in which the seal
Is set on how, by each man's latent nature taught,
He'll come to be and will be realized, not free
Of God, nor God of him, in Being's give and take.

And Destiny determines when and where and how
The Maker of your soul decided to allow
Your life to start and end, its context, nature, too.

Your pre-creation essence—heaven's 'latent you'—
That wants to be, determines the Determiner—
'Tis what the One Who's made in making must
    prefer.

(66) Ibn Arabi Tells of Jesus

If Jesus by the Lord's permission raised the dead
You'll do the same when to a seed conveying Light
By lifting up a fellow soul from deep despair
To life: you both are One in what it means to Be.

As favor to Himself, His breath, the Lord had fed
His not-yet-manifested Names with great delight
By answering their urgent preparation-pray'r
To rise and to reveal the Treasure that was He.

It has been claimed that when the Holy One delays
Before replying to the supplication of
A worshiper, He well may do it moved by love

To hear the heart-lent plea repeated. Every praise
He grants to you to utter, soul-devoted word,
Is given, that your hope, beloved, may be heard.

(67) Ibn Arabi Tells of Solomon

King Solomon the jinns and elemental pow'rs
Controlled to dig and build and forge. Bukhari told
About a demon who attempted to destroy
Muhammad in the night: He seized it and he tied

The villain to a pillar in a mosque. In hours
Of morning light the children played with it, so bold!
Great spirit-taming wisdom only they enjoy
Who deeply know the One where creature-lives abide.

Muhammad said, 'We sleep, and waken when we die.'
He meant: Our life is like a dream, and what we see
Is apparition, that interpreted must be.

Muhammad dreamed of drinking milk—of knowledge
   high
An emblem. Thus our prayer: 'May my knowledge
   grow.'
Becoming's real—and all imagined. This I know.

(68) Ibn Arabi Tells of David

The forest-mountains that uplifted higher were
In voice accordant with the Lord-appointed rise
Of him, Vice-regent made by heavenly command,
Will emblemize the empathy we, too, may feel.

We learn from the Qur'an that 'Bounty' would concur
As kindred gift to David. How to serve the skies
With aid that will conform to what we understand
In faithful keeping of our mirror of the Real?

The goal to which we all are rightly traveling
Conditions them who know and touch it inwardly—
It's been the deeper starting point, outpacing wrath:

We call it Godly Mercy. When a bird will sing
To greet King David we can hear it. When I see
The sign of 'softened iron,' I am on his path.

(69) Ibn Arabi Tells of Jonah

As Jonah safely had to life returned, reflect
On how to do the same. 'One evil's recompense'—
'Another evil, like it'? Don't retaliate,
Since claw-for-claw is evil. One who will forgive

Rewarded is by God and shall in favor live.
A human's in His image made. So virtue great
Accrues to one who'll save a life—his worth immense
Who Deity within us gladly will protect.

Man's multiple, not one in essence, while the Lord
Is unified in Being, though of many Names—
And when the God of Life entire remembrance
    claims,

We might—in part—forget . . . Let all your parts
    accord!
As God for Abraham cooled fire, in hell the flames
May well be cool and safe—compassion may afford.

(70) Ibn Arabi Tells of Job

We are the form of God, He's our Identity.
In each of us, an angel-animal, awakes
A six-directional awareness. World-mapped four,
Plus up and down, proclaim: we face Him
   everywhere.

And yet the world is not equilibrated. He
A love may show unique, supreme. Then torment
   takes
A role predominating for awhile. When sore
In heart, we're not commanded silently to bear

A woe like that of Job. God's pained within the form
Of any human that is hurt. We beg relief
From what is both a lower and a Higher grief.

The cosmos tranquil balance can't achieve. A storm
Enlivens, or may kill, or teach. A prophet knows
The Healer nearer comes, entreated in our woes.

(71) Ibn Arabi Tells of John the Baptist

John's name in Arabic is Yaḥya, 'He That Lives'—
No human being ever bore that name before:
It emblemized the high delight the father knew—
A son had come, at last, from God for him to love.

When Zachariah prayed, the Holy One Who Gives
Rewarded him. Like those the Lord had heard
    implore
In former times, like Sarah, Hannah, in the view
Of God he merited the succor from above.

When 'Give me from Yourself an heir' the father said,
He named the Lord before the object of his dream—
So Pharaoh's wife had done, entreating, 'Build for me

With You a dwelling in Your Paradise.' We see
The way they heaven's boon requested would beseem
Their deep, heart-uttered plea that to His ear had
    sped.

(72) Ibn Arabi Tells of Zachariah

The would-be father well-rewarded in his moan
Informed the world concerning Mercy. Naught could
  be
Created, were it lacking. Better to exist
Than not—each essence, every Name that gift will
  need.

A mercy may be earned in giving charity
Or doing other duties the Qur'an can list—
Or it may granted be by heaven-grace alone.
The Lord enfolds in Mercy: let the hearer heed.

Creation-Breath which had the Yearner's want
  relieved
May be accounted Mercy to His heart, aggrieved
When He, the Treasure, to no creature yet was
  known.

The unawake, to Mercy too accustomed grown,
Will beg for it to come, and speedily, through pray'r.
Say rather, 'Mercy let remain!' For it is there.

(73) Ibn Arabi Tells of Elias

Elias, who had earlier been put on earth
In form of Idris, may a double doctrine send.
When in that former body, he the station gained
Where nothing but his animality he knew.

He could not speak of it, made mute in second birth
To that awareness, yet may now the lesson lend
That you, God's creature, have a blessed gift attained
Deserving gratitude, the spirit to renew.

Elias, in his later shape, a vision saw:
Mount Lebanon split open to reveal a steed
Caparisoned in flame. He riding, felt that all

The lust within was gone. Pure intellect, in awe,
He felt himself to be, a state of pow'r—and need:
'Transcend both mind and body!' is our heaven-call.

(74) Ibn Arabi Tells of Luqmān

Luqmān, for wisdom famed in the Qur'an, had urged:
'My son, regard this tiny mustard seed, which God
Would into being bring if it indeed were hid
Within a rock, in heaven or the depths of earth.'

We know it is the Lord Who would have thus
    emerged
From starry flame or adamant 'neath sand or sod.
And why? He's in the world Himself, he dwells amid
The interstellar treasures of galactic birth.

The germ will nourish Him as it may nourish you:
Your latent nature in essential form He knows
And so the Knower can become. The light that grows

Within that uncreated seed will burst to view
When, having nourished Heav'n, the earth 'twill
    nourish too:
The micro-sun that sown is known delighted glows.

(75) Ibn Arabi Tells of Aaron

To burn the golden calf there wasn't any need,
As learnéd Aaron showed to Moses: 'Calm your
    wrath.'
Mere form, though glorified, is transient and will
    pass:
The calf would perish on its own—all rage in vain.

Divinity will eager seekers only feed
With lofty thought if it can place them on the path
Where passion will advance. Who passion can amass
Will understand the grandeur of creative gain.

We're all, in worship, subject to the reign of time—
All objects venerated manifest the Lord.
Whatever we adore may thus unfolded be

Upon the level of the spirit-station we
Have reached, and with our passion-level must
    accord.
The Face of Him is everywhere—though veiled,
    Sublime.

(76) Ibn Arabi Tells of Moses: Manifold Wisdom

The Hebrew boys whom Pharaoh, tyrant-minded,
   slew
Did not entirely perish: every infant life,
With purity of all the pre-created souls
That to the primal call for Trust replied, "We're
   Yours"

Were made to live in Moses' heart: to him they flew,
And each to him would bring, unsullied by the strife,
A latent nature open to the spirit-goals
For which the Lord prepared it, Whom no ill
   immures.

The treasures that the liberating prophet may
To me, awaiting, in their plenitude convey
Are manifold, and in my song, if Heaven wills,

Will be included what Divine desire fulfills.
Be blest whatever here my spirit-hymn distills:
Indeed I never spoke of this before today.

موسی

(77) Ibn Arabi Tells of Moses: Rain and Youth

The Prophet loved the feeling of the rain upon
His head uncovered: fresh from God the drops would
    fall,
And each a herald, to his Being lent to bring
A letter sent directly from the Trusted One.

The way the active powers coming from the dawn
Of Moses' youth would work was like the pleasant
    call
Of younger self to older: playing, chattering
With boyhood new-embodied, he would feel a sun

Of warmth toward the child, a will to guide, protect
The soul much nearer to the Lord from Whom he'd
    come
Like freshened rain, in contact with his God, direct—

The older Moses, not superior, indeed,
To this, the younger self, replete with halidom,
A helpful emissary: lead him, hear, and heed!

(78) Ibn Arabi Tells of Moses: River Basket

The river basket that the infant boy contained
Can represent his human nature—and the stream
He floated on, the body-learning he acquired
By thought and feeling and imagining, the ways

He learned direction and the guiding spirit gained
Capacity to be the vessel-captain. Theme
Of import, here—for so Reality desired
To lead the cosmic boat, the faithful heart amaze.

The basket: image of destruction? Outwardly—
But innnerly it meant the child escaped from death.
So Moses, like the world, will by the Names be led

'Mid ways and waves aquiver, chaos-buffeted,
Bewildered while they swell—the Being in our breath
Brave, unabating guide to new perplexity.

(79) Ibn Arabi Tells of Moses: Asiyah and Pharaoh

The basket halting by a tree at water's edge,
Asiyah, whom the Lord had for perfection made,
Inspired by thought divine, her husband Pharaoh
    urged
A mercy to exert, and save the boy. She said,

Removing tenderly the vessel from the sedge,
'Let him a consolation be for us,' and laid
The baby in a bed of safety, who emerged
From peril so, by kindly heart to comfort led.

He'd later benefit the monarch when he turned
The latter's mind to recognize the Only Lord,
Who took him in the act of this commitment, so

Although the Pharaoh drowned, the God for Whom
    he yearned
Was gained, the kingly soul in radiant accord
With Will Divine, a holy end to worldly woe.

(80) Ibn Arabi Tells of Khālid ibn Sinān

Though not enjoined to prophethood, yet Khālid
  thought
The faith of hearers in their Messengers would be
In grateful manner strengthened if he should confirm
That what they'd said while on the earth was true
  and just.

He, in the space 'tween death and judgment, wanted
  taught
The lesson that I mentioned, and accordingly
Intended to convey that mercy in his term
Of dwelling in the afterworld, as spirits must.

The heritage he left is one of wise intent
Although it isn't clear that he the lesson lent
Was to the people quite permitted to proclaim.

And yet we know he took great pleasure, all the
  same,
In having lived so near the time Muhammad dwelt
Upon the earth, and gladdened by compassion felt.

(81) Ibn Arabi Tells of Muhammad: Syzygy

God, man, and woman—three aligned, a syzygy.
The Lord gave man His image, then from man he
　　drew
The latter's image, woman. Man for God must long,
His origin; and woman, likewise for the man—

And God loves man, man woman as the Deity
Loves *him*. The loving union of the mortal two
Will be annihilation of the self—that strong!
Though God is jealous, a complete ablution can

Re-purify the man to view Him in the one
In whom he'd been annihilated. That is done
Because—a truth, be sure, Muhammad, loving,
　　knew—

To contemplate a woman with a zeal Divine
Is to perceive the Real embodied in a sign:
God rightly gives to every creature what is due.

(82) Ibn Arabi Tells of Muhammad: Triads

Muhammad said he'd come to love and value three
Attractions highly: women and perfúme and pray'r,
The middle item masculine in gender and
The two that frame it feminine—triplicity

That mirrors neatly Woman, Man, and Essence. We
In Godly Essence and in woman are aware
Of female-gendered nouns arranged on either hand,
The masculine enframing: God-engendered, he;

She, filled with Godly grace beloved by the man.
The feminine prevails. If God's the 'Cause,' we can,
Again, discover here a female-gendered noun.

And as for sweet perfúme, we gladly find the crown
Of fragrance in aromas linked to generation
In women when embraced with loving exultation.

(83) Ibn Arabi Tells of Muhammad: 'The Opening'

Three verses open the Qur'an. Of God they chant:
'May He be praised, the Lord of worlds, Beneficent
And Merciful, the Owner of the Judgment Day.'
The focus here is on the Highest, Him alone.

The central thought is 'You we worship, You we ask
For help,' and here the Lord and we, the worshipers,
Proclaim an interchange: we ask, and He will grant.
Three verses, hoping we may walk on favored path

And straight, not that of strayers who engender
    wrath,
Are centering on us. A symmetry is lent:
Throughout the opening, to Him, the Great, we pray;

Throughout the final part, we beg to stay His own.
The middle line allotted God and us a task:
We aid receive the way the Merciful prefers.

(84) Ibn Arabi Tells of Muhammad: The 'Last Name' of God

There's unity of Being: God and world are one,
And when you pray to Him, we're told He prays with
    you.
But who is He that prays? The Hidden Being? No,
The God of your belief is coming to your aid—

The God Whom you, by the imagining you've done,
By thinking, contemplating, hold in spirit-view—
Whom wisdom of your late attainment-state may
    show.
And He Who knows you knows the self you've lately
    made.

In prayer you address Him by His Name 'the Last,'
The latest form that now the Lord will ably take
Upon the level where your spirit may awake.

For we, as well, are formed by what we have amassed
In wisdom and in love, that we can render back:
We lag behind the leader on the racing track.

(85) Ibn Arabi Tells of the Substitute

A silence of the mouth and heart will aid
A hermitlike withdrawal: these may quell
The thought of self, make room for God. Then add
A hunger, vigilance, and wakeful wait.

With quiet, fast, retreat, and waking made
Aware of every minute, one may well
Discern a fourfold knowing can be had
Of God, soul, world and Satan. You, elate,

Move onward, to an angel-nature new
Reshaped, are Substitute—the older 'you'
Replaced. In the location where you'd stayed

A soul who'd will to glimpse you now might view
Your gladder nature bodied forth, a true
Envisioning, the spirit-real portrayed.

Prayers

(86) Ibn Arabi's Prayer: Sunday Evening

Though 'I' converse with 'You,' the Universal 'He'
Are You as well, and I, who in Your form was made,
Implore to be Your mirror-light, the One reflect:
Third person, hidden Root, my coessential Heart.

Unknowable, Unwordable eternally,
The 'He' Unlimited—yet limited, inlaid
Within me in a way transcending intellect,
At one with deepest Being whence it cannot part.

Eliminate the blood-speck of unworthiness
From my imperfect heart as You the herald lent
To take the particle that Iblis yet might claim

From out the Prophet's heart, whom gratefully we
    bless:
With angel-purified resplendent element
Of holy Being he invoked the Sacred Name.

(87) Ibn Arabi's Prayer: Sunday Morning

When God unveils, there is no other. When He veils,
Then all is other, each is a concealed adored.
Though You're the hidden Being, yet as Many-Named
We know You, and through every thing—that hides
   Your light

When I consider it a thing, for thinghood fails—
All separation halts before the Open-Doored.
My soul would praise You daily. Be the more
   acclaimed,
Who are extolled when beings, breathing, feel Your
   Might.

I ask You, bless the guide-reciter whom we hear,
Whose heart You have illumined by the crystaled
   flame—
The places where the full moon climbs, and starlight
   shines

From heaven-lamp afar regarded—friend brought
   near.
Let not existence veil me from my praise-borne claim
Of witness to the One that Maker-form divines.

(88) Ibn Arabi's Prayer: Monday Evening

By Your high Name and merciful, on me bestow
A heart wherein sublimer aspirations ask
And one to which disdainful spirits may be led,
That I may comfort give and tranquil strength and
    calm—

Embracing all, in knowledge and compassion grow,
As You, Who every moment are upon some task,
Are manifested everywhere. May I, with longing fed
And fear of You, Revered, the blessing of Your balm

Acknowledge hourly. As, upon the birth of John,
Elizabeth and Zachariah felt the dawn
Of hope and awe and, joyful, hastened to the good,

So let me not forget what I have understood:
The nearness of Your voice will daily be my joy,
As fragrance of sweet basil hailed the prophet-boy.

(89) Ibn Arabi's Prayer: Monday Morning

Unchain me from the bonds of limited belief:
Dispersive whim-frivolity, constricting rigor.
Unveil me, loose the knots of doubt and supposition,
Of calculation as of apathy, and stand-out pride.

I narrowness would leave behind, unneeded grief:
A refuge from myself in You I seek with vigor.
My 'self' annihilate! I pray for manumission
From crushing weight of 'me' that sullen pined and
    sighed.

I flee from You to You, for there's no 'I' apart
From Him Who is alone my Being and my Heart:
In micro-world I mirror You That have no end.

I also fly from You to You, high-riddling Friend,
In willing to forget the ruse that made it seem
As if apart from You my self were more than dream.

(90) Ibn Arabi's Prayer: Tuesday Evening

I would entreat You, by Your Name 'The Forceful,'
   Most
Tremendous in Your course to conquer, elevate
My soul to reach the Lote Tree of my bound extreme,
Then let me afterward as orbit-cycle feel

The upward complemented by the downward—host
Of energies upraise me to a high estate,
Aware of Origin to soar, then, falling, dream,
Renewed, though separate, of the Unending Real.

There is no aptitude for the originated
To bear the Pre-Existent. When I'm grasped and
   whirled
And so approach at last the Garden of Abode,

I feel the speeding light that in the seed You sowed
Your Being mirrors when the vision is unfurled
Of what I am in deepest longing, heart elated.

(91) Ibn Arabi's Prayer: Tuesday Morning

Two men of awe in white appeared in my retreat
Upon the Mount of Opening. One said, 'Let be
For each agreeing quester this my message.' They
Were Moses, Aaron, maybe—one the other's voice:

'Immerse me in the ocean, fathomless and sweet,
Unending water of Your Oneness' open sea.
May lightning-flashes, each a near and piercing ray
Of sky-compassion, find me: let my soul rejoice.

Invest me with the robe of Might, Acceptance. Clear
A path to lead me on to join and so attain.
And through Your radiant Name from light of all
   Your Names

Grant amplitude: may souls approach and find me
   dear.
Pour light into my heart: true shelter let me gain
Below Your canopy that Mercy-warmth enframes.'

(92) Ibn Arabi's Prayer: Wednesday Evening

Your Name of 'God' is master of the Names that tell
Your qualities, the single way they all will face,
Uniting realms of both Creation and Command.
O grant me that my thought be toward that center
  bent,

That I be focus of the gazes that impel
A testament, my wish and will dissolved in grace
Of Your bestowing. Then shall men the fiery brand
Of guiding get from me, as You to Moses lent

A flaming proof that Your dominion would record
To Pharaoh, who before he died would know the
  Lord.
And bless Muhammad, in the shelter of whose light

The burning bush was made to shine. Our Prophet
  soared
Astride Buraq to know the very heaven-height
Where angel, spirit lent him blessing by Your Might.

(93) Ibn Arabi's Prayer: Wednesday Morning

O Lord, Compassionate to Noah, Jonah, Job,
And Moses, cover up my errors with a veil,
My sins with Your Forgiveness: You will never seek
To burden any soul with more than it can bear.

With Mercifier-Will enclose me in a robe
Of Pardon: let my heart whose hope will never pale,
Whose nature is to change, be turned to the Unique
And Flowing Source of change in earth, fire, water,
   air.

The darkness of created objects pray dispel
That would erase the emblem-lesson each would tell:
Increase my knowledge, every atom of my Being

Help let me know in true symbolic mode of seeing.
With wisdom and with gnosis may I be endued
To feel beyond the seen what never can be viewed.

(94) Ibn Arabi's Prayer: Thursday Evening

Extend to me the present of the list'ning ear,
The quiet cave where we unveil the Hidden Source.
The Seven Sleepers, the Ephesians, who remained
In deep reclusion give the hint: when we withdraw

From outward manifold to heed the inner sphere,
No multiplicity can keep us from the deeper Force.
Detached, we contemplate; awakening, we've gained
The skill to hear the Language of our God in awe.

We comprehend: the world's a letter You have sent
To You—the Solomon, the Loved One. You have made
The loved ones who will read. The Lover will unlade

The lore of longing: we explore the Treasure meant
To be unburied, unconcealed, and gladly see
Encoded, Holy, the Supreme commandment: "Be!"

(95) Ibn Arabi's Prayer: Thursday Morning

God, let me be extinguished in Your contemplation,
Annihilated in Your Being. So when Moses prayed
That he might see the Lord, he learned how this
   might be:
'That mountain—should it stay in place, I will
   appear.'

The mount was so bestirred by God in lofty station
That it was crushed, and was a helpful emblem
   made:
Let self be disregarded, vanish utterly:
'Tis only then you come to know: the Lord is here.

When Moses humbly asked, 'What love You most, O
   King?'
He said, 'That you in every state remember Me.'
My spirit of remembrance—let it lifted be

To join the Highest of Assemblies 'round Your throne.
The one who God remembers when he is alone—
Him will the Lord remember, and to Heaven bring.

(96) Ibn Arabi's Prayer: Friday Evening

Lord, teach me of Your Names the ones you find most
    right
For Your dictation. I indeed remember well
That when our father Adam all 'the Names' had told
To all the angels, they fell prostrate in amaze.

What was the nature of the Names he'd then recite?
Interpreters there are who'd confidently tell
The questioner: 'Each was an angel-name enscrolled
On Adam's widened mind: they merit startled praise.'

Muhammad took dictation from an angel kind.
But God, replenished from the Name 'Nonmanifest,'
Taught Adam not the angel-names but thought it
    best

That He should learn the Names of God Himself,
    and so
Be Perfect Man in skiey gnosis, giv'n to grow
In love, that ever more potential he might find.

(97) Ibn Arabi's Prayer: Friday Morning

Make me Your *álif* in detachment, single line,
And fill my heart and mind with love and wise regard
For all that You have made, and I'll the inkwell be
Wherefrom the cosmic writing pen You may supply.

Within my mirror-soul Your Jewel-Names let shine,
That if oppressor, man or jinn, with feelings hard,
Should in presumption plot, and evil mean for me,
Reflected gems would burn that thought and it would
    die.

There is an aspect to the self that may command
The spirit to commit a wrong—this I'd subdue.
Yea, even Joseph, chaste and pure, could understand

That urge, and felt it quelled by Mercy come from
    You.
Invest me with an angel-strength to curb the sway
Of any thought that turns me from Your Face away.

(98) Ibn Arabi's Prayer: Saturday Evening

You stations for our spirit-journey have ordained
And stages have arranged for our pursuit of good—
And as the mansions of the moon are ordered by
Her altered light, more near or farther from the Sun,

So I will light and dark encounter, pleased or pained,
And hope that value I'll have learned as best I could.
I pray that nothing may obscure from me Your high
Design inscribed in every atom, action done.

My attribute is possibility, my goad—
My substance, non-existing—and my real abode
Is poverty. My refuge only is to view

My doings from the standpoint, Holy God, of You.
With brilliance of Your Light my hidden life unveil,
And school me to allude to what will never fail.

(99) Ibn Arabi's Prayer: Saturday Morning

For seven gifts I thank You on the seventh day:
An Abram-angel into Your serene preserve
Of deep benevolence I came. And then the garden
Of Your compassion, Moses-like, I entered, blest.

Your love I felt, as Moses did, a child away
From parents' home. Like Jesus, me Your Name
    would serve
With bounty from the table spread in Godly pardon.
And as to Adam, Noah, Jacob, Isaac, best

Of grace to me You gave, Your law to honor. Wells
I drank from, as the maidens did at Midian. You
Have clothed me in the robe of servant ever true.

I lastly pray the Prophet who Your will fulfilled
Be my example of the faith You have instilled:
Let daily confidence be praised, as he impels.

Three Mystic Odes by Ibn Arabi

"Equal Worth of All Religions" by Ibn Arabi

1) You doves, that 'round the Egypt-willow, thorn-tree float,
My yearning-pain don't double through your cooing dirge.

2) Have mercy! You will never lure, with loud complaint,
My feelings rooted deep in sadness, longing, want.

3) I morn and evening answer you the same—with moan
Of one who longs and loves, the plaint of one in love.

4) 'Mid tamarinds in swampy thicket, spirits stood
Around me, boughs to bend, my self to nihilate.

5) They brought me varied versions of my longing-woe
And of impassioned love, and rare, unwonted tests.

6) Who'll grant me certainty, the union to attain,
The stone-throw and the source, nobility and bliss?

7) My heart they compassed, rousing love and lover's pain.
Above the veil, they kissed my elements of life.

8) Muhammad, best of creatures, 'round the Kaaba stone
Proceeded, teaching: intellect is incomplete.

9) Though prophet, stones he kissed. But what can valued be
In Mecca temple, next to worth of humankind?

10) How often women promised faithfulness to vows—
But vow-fulfilment one with henna'd hand disdained.

11) Among best wonder-things the veiled gazelle I find,
Red finger signaling and eyelid winking sly.

12) Her grazing place—between the breast and entrails. Fine
This garden situated 'midst the lively fires!

13) My heart must welcome every form—for the gazelle
A grazing place, a convent for the Christian monks.

14) An idol temple; for the pilgrim, Kaaba-shrine;
The Torah tablets and the scroll of the Qur'an.

15) For mine is the religion of a mystic love,
And where its camel leads, my faith will travel, too.

16) That love had Bisch'r, whom both Hind and sister loved,
And also Kaïs, Laila, Maija and Gailán.

"Vision of the Divine Being" by Ibn Arabi

1) In gently sloping vale between two cliffs will be
The meeting. Let our camels here find resting place
And drink their fill, for thus we end our weary day.

2) Seek nothing farther than such humble travel-goal,
And ask for nothing more when we have reached the spot:
Here graze, good camels: Bárik, Hágir, and Tahmad!

3) And give yourselves to play as do the friendly girls
With gently swelling breasts. Enjoy the opulence
Of grassland, in the mood of feminine gazelles.

4) Upon the meadow swarmed and hummed the welcome bees.
The chirping birds, the merrymakers, would reply.

5) The meadow soil, how soft! And soft the fanning wind—
With lightnings cloudy-veiled and thunders cloudwhite-hid.

6) The raindrops from the rifts in cloud fall down like
    tears
A lover sheds on parting from the one he loves.

7) Drink fully of the tincture-cup of mystic love
Inebriating and, ecstatic, hear the voice
Of one who gently, tenderly, will birdlike sing:

8) "O wine so pure, you in the age of Adam told
A tale that, certain and secure, would paradise
Portray, the place of dwelling made for humankind.

9) Fair maidens from their spicebox would permit to
    fall
Your musky drops; and modest virgins, perfect
    pearls,
The wine for us decanted in a selfless way."

"Apotheosis of the Human" by Ibn Arabi

1) O ancient temple that you are! A light for you
Awakens that in both our hearts together shines.

2) I must bewail to you the wasteland I have crossed
And where, in streamings unconfined, I tears have shed.

3) Not morn or evening could I know the bliss of rest—
From morningtide to eve unstopping did I walk.

4) My camels move at night although with wounded feet—
Indeed, their eager tread is even faster then.

5) These mighty riding-camels carried us to You
With deep desire—they hadn't hoped to reach the goal.

6) They lovestruck hastened on the wild and rainless way
Nor of their weariness would think to voice complaint.

7) They never wailed for pain of heavy love. 'Twas I
Who moaned of tiredness—I, with contradiction filled.

Appendix

from *Art Bridges: The Beauty of God in Calligraphy*
Shahid Alam, Calligraphy Exhibition at
St. Catherine's Cathedral, Hamburg, Germany
3 October to 5 November 2015 14–15

Art Bridges: The Beauty of God in Calligraphy
Introduction by Shahid Alam
tr. MB

In Baghdad, in the House of Wisdom (Arabic: Bayt-al-Ḥikma) during the ninth century of our era, the most important works of antiquity were translated from Greek into Arabic. In this way, the most significant exponents of Hellenistic antiquity and of scientific achievements later in Toledo came to be translated, in turn, from Arabic into Latin and thereby preserved for European scientific culture, becoming available also in the various vernaculars of Europe. This cultural transfer would have been unthinkable without the achievement of Arabic writing with its particular forms of language and style.

Our focus here is on the aesthetic of Arabic script. Today as then, its beauty can help us, in a way that constantly renews our awareness, to experience and to cross the bridge from and to each other. On this journey—as in Lessing's play *Nathan the Wise* or in Halévy's opera *The Jewish Woman*—one may recognize the foreign in a way that brings it home and leads to interreligious dialogue, to intercultural understanding. In present-day Europe, and not least in Germany, cultural diversity, along with the cherishing of its individual components, is valued. Today's political situation, in all its urgency, shows that such an enthusiasm cannot be taken for granted, but is a cultural achievement and necessity in need of continual renewal. During the time I spoke of—about twelve centuries ago—Arabic script proved a bridge to scientific development. Today—in the present exhibition—that script should be regarded as an aesthetic bridge to intercultural dialogue.

For "God is beautiful and He loves beauty"—as we learn from a celebrated saying attributed to the Prophet, which has been given suitably beautiful presentation in many calligraphies. Or we may remember Schiller: "Only through Beauty's eastern gate / May you enter the Knowledge Land." Through the aesthetic of Arabic script and the art of Islamic calligraphy, hearts may become open to the beauty of God; the bridge that leads to knowledge may be crossed; intercultural understanding and interreligious dialogue may be fostered.

Since the summer of 2005 twenty exhibitions have presented my work to the public in Catholic and Lutheran churches nationwide. The idea of exhibiting Islamic art and Arabic calligraphy in Christian churches has not always been deemed self-evidently desirable. The churches that opened their gates to Islamic art took a great and brave step forward. To view the other, to see the other in oneself, to develop a feeling for the specialness of the other, revives a memory of the earlier sacred space in a Bayt-al-Ḥikma, a House of Wisdom.

The public observed with astonishment that Bishop Heinrich Mussinghoff inaugurated my exhibition at St. Peter's Cathedral at Aachen in 2007 with a lecture on the first line of "The Opening" (*Al-Fatiḥa*), the first sura or chapter of the Qur'an. The overwhelming number of visitors at all of my exhibitions indicates that a broad public eagerly welcomes such an initiative. "Given the present-day world situation, the need for religious dialogue is today more pressing than ever. History belongs to those who bring together what had been separated, who travel paths of life that had hitherto been barred" (K.-J. Kuschel, *Living is Bridge Building*, 2011).

It is the special aesthetic of Arabic script that also fascinated great poets such as Goethe and that serves as the basis for this exhibition. In a letter of 1815 Goethe praised Arabic script in these words: "In no language, perhaps, are spirit, word, and script together embodied in such a primal, original way."

The center of gravity for this exhibition is provided by calligraphically represented texts from Torah, Gospel, and Qur'an on large wooden tablets (210 cm x 75 cm). The observer is invited to a thoughtful consideration of the shared content of the three as well as the differences.

The bronze word sculpture ILM—meaning "Knowledge" and "Wisdom"—opens a new direction in the art of calligraphy. Liberated from a two-dimensional background, it stands freely in open space. You can see from all sides how the three letters, the three root consonants (*'ain-lam-mim*), are welded together and make the transition from triplicity to unity.

The three-meter wooden sculpture Alif, in a space surrounded by other works, emblemizes what is shared in the alphabets of all three holy scriptures. For the alphabets of the three great Mediterranean writing cultures each begin with an Alif or Aleph or Alpha. Correspondingly, the Alif can serve as central axis or juncture point within a triptych: at one side the first sura of the Qur'an, *Al-Fatiḥa*, at the other side the "Our Father" or, as Arabic-speaking Christians call it, the *Abana*.

Calligraphically represented poetic excerpts from great poets and mystics such as Goethe, Rilke, Hölderlin, Mansur al-Hallaj—in Arabic translation and also in the original languages—build a further bridge for the observer. Translations from Arabic poems to German and from German poems to Arabic are literal (letter-made) bridges to other shores. Not only the artistic setting of the Arabic texts but also their content is important for the understanding of an art that seeks to build a bridge between East and West and thereby to come a bit nearer to the vision of Friedrich Rückert: "World poetry alone is world conciliation."

Artist Shahid Alam, born 1952 in Lahore, Pakistan, has lived in Germany since 1973. He studied pedagogy, art, and political science with a European focus and was active for more than 20 years in the areas of education and art. Since 1996 he has worked as freelance artist not far from Aachen.

Source Notes

xliv. "Boundless Love." I translate these lines from a German rendering by the great Islamologist Annenarie Schimmel, to which my attention was first directed by Shahid Alam:
Mein Herz ward fähig, jede Form zu tragen,
Gazellenweide, Kloster wohlgelehrt,
Ein Götzentempel, Ka'ba eines Pilgers,
Der Thora Tafeln, der Koran geehrt:
Ich folg' der Religion der Liebe, wo auch
Ihr Reittier zieht, hab' ich mich hingekehrt.
(See Schimmel, *Mystische Dimensionen* 384.)

Poem 1. For the secret sadness of the longing sigh of God, Who yearns that His treasure be revealed, see Corbin, *AwA* 115, 128–129. Ibn Arabi tells us that God says, "I was a Treasure but was not known. So I loved to be known, and I created the creatures and made Myself known to them. Then they came to know Me." (*Meccan Openings* II 231.33, 232. 1, qtd. in *SPK* 66; *SPK* 86–90 for more on Treasuries). For "con-spiration" and compassion see *AwA* 145.

Poem 2. *AwA* 63, 130–131, 142, 158, 247.

Poem 3. Qur'an 28:88. ". . . Everything will perish save His countenance." Cf. *AwA* 244. For Muhammad's vision of Gabriel see *AwA* 80, 217, 219, 223–224, 231. For Queen of Sheba and mirror-floor see Qur'an 27:44. For the container metaphor see *SPK* 127, 134.

Poem 4. For Fatima, Adam, Eve, Mary, Christ, and Sophiology see *AwA* 40, 161–163; for al-Khidr *AwA* 61–65.
Poem 5. Chittick, *SPK* 323.
Poem 6. *SPK* 119–123, esp. 122, also 126–128.
Poem 7. *SPK* 119, 126–126, 365.
Poem 8. *SPK* 202–203.
Poem 9. *SPK* 276–278.
Poem 10. *SPK* 118.
Poem 11. *SPK* 320–321.
Poem 12. *AwA* 259–260.
Poem 13. *SPK* 355.
Poem.14. *SPK* 217–218.
Poem 15. *SPK* 98–99.
Poem 16. *SPK* 221–222.
Poem 17. *SPK* 365, 119.
Poem 18. *SPK* 158.
Poem 19. *SPK* 320.
Poem 20. *SPK* 105–106.
Poem 21. *SPK* 20–21.
Poem 22. *SPK* 152.
Poem 23. *SPK* 280–281.
Poem 24. *SPK* 341–343.
Poem 25. *SPK* 352–353.
Poem 26. *SPK* 338–339.
Poem 27. *SPK* 106–108.
Poem 28. *SPK* 194.
Poem 29. *SPK* 378–379.
Poem 30. *SPK* 301–303.
Poem 31. *SPK* 100, 395.
Poem 32. *SPK* 91–92.
Poem 33. *SPK* 184–185.
Poem 34. *SPK* 55–56.
Poem 35. *SPK* 174–175.
Poem 36. *SPK* 211.
Poem 37. *SPK* 215.
Poem 38. *SPK* 267.

Poem 39. *SPK* 118.
Poem 40. *SPK* 368–369.
Poem 41. *SPK* 299.
Poem 42. *SPK* 61–62.
Poem 43. *SPK* 86–87, 90.
Poem 44. *SPK* 140.
Poem 45. *SPK* 53–54.
Poem 46. *SPK* 86.
Poem 47. *SPK* 223.
Poem 48. Chittick, *SDG* 175.
Poem 49. *SDG* 170.
Poem 50. *SDG* 236–237.
Poem 51. *SDG* 122–123..
Poem 52. *BW* 50–57.
Poem 53. *BW* 61–68.
Poem 54. *BW* 73–81.
Poem 55. *BW* 85–87.
Poem 56. *BW* 90–95.
Poem 57. *BW* 99–103.
Poem 58. *BW* 106–110.
Poem 59. *BW* 113–118.
Poem 60. *BW* 122–127.
Poem 61. *BW* 128–138.
Poem 62. *BW* 141–144.
Poem 63. *BW* 146–153.
Poem 64. *BW* 156–162.
Poem 65. *BW* 163–171.
Poem 66. *BW* 179–186.
Poem 67. *BW* 196–197.
Poem 68. *BW* 198–205.
Poem 69. *BW* 208–211.
Poem 70. *BW* 212–217.
Poem 71. *BW* 218–221.
Poem 72. *BW* 222–227.
Poem 73. *BW* 228–235.
Poem 74. *BW* 236–240.

Poem 75. *BW* 242–248.
Poem 76. *BW* 251–252.
Poem 77. *BW* 252.
Poem 78. *BW* 251–254.
Poem 79. *BW* 254–255.
Poem 80. *BW* 267–268.
Poem 81. *BW* 274–275.
Poem 82. *BW* 277–278.
Poem 83. *BW* 280–284, *AwA* 249–257.
Poem 84. *BW* 282–283.
Poem 85. *FPST* 23, 27–40.
Poem 86. *SDH* 25–26.
Poem 87. *SDH* 27–32.
Poem 88. *SDH* 33–34.
Poem 89. *SDH* 35–38.
Poem 90. *SDH* 39–40.
Poem 91. *SDH* 41–42.
Poem 92. *SDH* 43–45.
Poem 93. *SDH* 47–48.
Poem 94. *SDH* 49–50.
Poem 95. *SDH* 62–56.
Poem 96. *SDH* 57–59.
Poem 97. *SDH* 61–63.
Poem 98. *SDH* 65–67.
Poem 99. *SDH* 69–71.
"Equal Worth . . ." *MT* 6–7.
"Vision . . ." *MT* 12–13.
"Deification . . ." *MT* 16.

Bibliography

Abrahamov, Binyamin. *Ibn al-'Arabi and the Sufis*. Oxford: Anqa Publishing, 2014.

Addas, Claude. *Quest for the Red Sulphur: The Life of Ibn 'Arabī*. Translated by Peter Kingsley. Cambridge: The Islamic Texts Society, 1993.

Alam, Shahid. "Kunstbrücken: Die Schönheit Gottes in der Kalligraphie." *Kunstbrücken. Die Schönheit Gottes in der Kalligraphie: Eine Ausstelling von Shahid Alam in der Hauptkirche St. Katharinen, Hamburg 3. Oktober bis 1. November 2015,* 14–15. No date or place of publication: Nordliche Weltweit, Zentrum für Mission und Ökumene.

Bidney, Martin. *Blake and Goethe: Psychology, Ontology, Imagination*. Columbia MO: University of Missouri Press, 1988.

Bidney, Martin. *East-West Poetry: A Western Poet Responds to Islamic Tradition in Sonnets, Hymns, and Songs*. East-West Bridge Builders Volume I. Albany: State University of New York Press, 2009.

Bidney, Martin. *Poems of Wine and Tavern Romance: A Dialogue with the Persian Poet Hafiz* (= PWTR). Translated by Bidney with verse replies. East-West Bridge Builders Volume III. Albany: State University of New York Press, 2013.

Blake, William. *The Complete Poetry & Prose of William Blake*. Newly revised edition. Edited by David V. Erdman. Commentary by Harold Bloom. New York: Doubleday, 1988.

Chittick, William C. *Imaginal Worlds: Ibn al-'Arabi and the Problem of Religious Diversity* [= IW]. Albany: State University of New York Press, 1994.

Chittick, William C. *The Self-Disclosure of God: Principles of Ibn al-'Arabī's Cosmology* [= *SDG*]. Albany: State University of New York Press, 1998. Contains many long passages from Ibn Arabi's *The Meccan Openings,* often called *The Meccan Revelations.*

Chittick, William C. *The Sufi Path of Knowledge: Ibn al-'Arabi's Metaphysics of Imagination* [= *SPK*]. Albany: State University of New York Press, 1989. Contains many long passages from Ibn Arabi's *The Meccan Openings*, often called *The Meccan Revelations.*

Corbin, Henry. *Alone with the Alone: Creative Imagination in the Sūfism of Ibn 'Arabi.* [= *AwA*]. No translator attribution. Preface by Harold Bloom. Bollingen Series XCI. Princeton: Princeton University Press, 1997.

Corbin, Henry. *Avicenna and the Visionary Recital.* Translated by Willard. R. Trask. Dallas: Spring Publications, 1980.

Corbin, Henry. *Swedenborg and Esoteric Islam.* Translated by Leonard Fox. West Chester PA: Swedenborg Foundation, 1999.

Emerson, Ralph Waldo. *The Works of Ralph Waldo Emerson.* Edited by George Sampson. London: G. Bell and Sons. 5 vols. Vol. 1: *Essays* and *Representative Men*, 1919.

Gaudin, C., editor and translator. *On Poetic Imagination and Reverie: Selections from the Words of Gaston Bachelard.* Indianapolis and New York: Bobbs Merrill, 1971.

Goethe, Johann Wolfgang von. *West-East Divan: The Poems, with "Notes and Essays": Goethe's Intercultural Dialogues* [= *WED*]. Translated with Commentary Poems by Martin Bidney. Translation of "Notes and Essays" assisted by Peter Anton von Arnim. East-West Bridge Builders Volume II. Albany: State University of New York Press, 2010.

Huizinga, Johan. *The Waning of the Middle Ages.* New York: Doubleday, 1954.

Ibn al 'Arabi. *The Bezels of Wisdom* [= *BW*]. Translation and Introduction by R. W. J. Austin. Preface by Titus Burckhardt. Classics of Western Spirituality. Mahwah NJ: Paulist Press, 1980.

Ibn al 'Arabi. *Contemplation of the Holy Mysteries and the Rising of the Divine Lights.* Translated by Cecilia Twinch and Pablo Beneito. Oxford: Anqa Publishing, 2008.

Ibn al 'Arabi. *The Four Pillars of Spiritual Transformation* [= *FPST*]. Translated by Stephen Hirtenstein. Oxford: Anqa Publishing, 2008.

Ibn al 'Arabi. *Journey to the Lord of Power: A Sufi Manual on Retreat* [= *JLP*]. Introduction by Sheikh Muzaffer Ozak al-Jerrahi. Notes from a Commentary by 'Abdul-Karim Jili. Translated by Rabia Terri Harris. Rochester VT: Inner Traditions International, 1989.

Ibn al 'Arabi. *The Meccan Revelations*. Volume I. Edited by Michael Chodkiewicz. Translated by William C. Chittick and James W. Morris. New York: Pir Press, 2005.

Ibn al 'Arabi. *The Meccan Revelations*. Volume II. Edited by Michael Chodkiewicz. Translated by Cyrille Chodkiewicz and Denis Gril. New York: Pir Press, 2004.

Ibn 'Arabi. *Mystische Texte aus dem Islam: drei Gedichte des Arabi, 1240;—Primary Source Edition* [= *MT*]. Translated and Interpreted by M. Horten. Bonn: A. Marcus und E. Weber's Verlag, 1912. Nabu Public Domain Reprints.

Ibn 'Arabī. *The Seven Days of the Heart: prayers for the nights and days of the week* [= *SDH*]. Translated and presented in English by Pablo Beneito and Stephen Hirtenstein. Oxford: Anqa Publications, 2008.

Jones, Mary McAllester. *Gaston Bachelard, Subversive Humanist: Texts and Readings*. Madison: University of Wisconsin Press, 1991.

Pickthall, Marmaduke. *The Meaning of the Glorious Koran: An Explanatory Translation*. New York: Knopf, 1992 (orig. pub. 1930). The most beautiful rendering of the Qur'an into English.

Schimmel, Annemarie. *Mystische Dimensionen des Islam. Geschichte des Sufismus*. Dederichs Verlag, 1985.

Schimmel, Annemarie. *Rumi's World: The Life and Work of the Great Sufi Poet*. Boston: Shambhala, 1992.

Taruskin, Richard. *Music in the Early Twentieth Century. The Oxford History of Western Music* Vol 4. Oxford: Oxford University Press, 2010.

Treiger, Alexander. *Inspired Knowledge in Islamic Thought: Al-Ghazālī's theory of mystical cognition and its Avicennian foundation*. London and New York: Routledge, 2012.

Supplementary Bibliography

Studies in Epiphanology by Martin Bidney

"Fire, Flutter, Fall and Scatter: A Structure in the Epiphanies of Hawthorne's Tales." *Nathaniel Hawthorne's Tales: A Norton Critical Edition*, second edition. Edited by James McIntosh. New York: Norton, 2013, 507–524. Abridged rpt. from *Texas Studies in Literature and Language* 50.1 (Spring 2008): 58–89.

"Flame-Engulfing Storms and Seas of Darkness: Byron's Love-Death Epiphanies in Kristevan Context." *Interdisciplinary Literary Studies* 12.2 (Spring 2011): 97–125.

"Bright Blur, Blinding Light, Blank Page: The Epistemically Skeptical Epiphanies of Chekhov." *Slavic and East European Journal* 54.2 (Summer 2010): 272–296.

"Peace and Pathos in the Sea Epiphanies of Rupert Brooke: Contours of Narcissistic Desire." *English Literature in Transition 1880–1920* 48.3 (Fall 2005): 324–338.

"Double Darkness, Border of Bonelight: The Problem of Solipsism in Howard Nemerov's Epiphanies." *Interdisciplinary Literary Studies* 6.2 (Spring 2005): 24–46.

"Rage and Reparation in the Epiphanies of Edward Thomas: Dark-Bright Water, Grating Roar." *English Literature in Transition 1880–1920* 47.3 (Fall 2004): 292–310.

"Epiphany in Autobiography: The Quantum Changes of Dostoevsky and Tolstoy." *Journal of Clinical Psychology / In Session* 60.5 (May 2004): 471–480 [special issue: Quantum Changes].

"The Aestheticist Epiphanies of J. D. Salinger: Bright-Hued Circles, Spheres, and Patches; 'Elemental' Joy and Pain." *Short Story Criticism* (Detroit: Gale, 2004) 65: 327–335. Rpt. from *Style* 34.1 (2000): 117–131.

"The Secretive-Playful Epiphanies of Robert Frost: Solitude, Companionship, and the Ambivalent Imagination." *The Wadsworth Casebook for Reading, Research, and Writing. Robert Frost: A Collection of Poems.* Edited by Robert C. Petersen. Boston: Wadsworth, 2004, 54–61. Abridged rpt. from *Papers on Language and Literature* 53 (2002): 270–294.

"Water, Movement, Roundness: Epiphanies and History in Tolstoy's *War and Peace*." *Leo Tolstoy*. Edited with Introduction by Harold Bloom. Philadelphia: Chelsea P, 2003 (Bloom's Modern Critical Views), 147–164. Rpt. from *Patterns of Epiphany*. Carbondale: Southern Illinois UP, 1997, 154–171.

"'A Dream' as Key to a Reverie Pattern in Matthew Arnold: Interactions of Water and Fire." *Twentieth-Century Literary Criticism* (Detroit: Gale, 2003) 128: 80–88. Rpt. from *Victorian Poetry* 26.1–2 (1988): 45–60.

"Controlled Panic: Mastering the terrors of Dissolution and Isolation in Elizabeth Bishop's Epiphanies." *Style* 34 (Spring 2000): 117–131.

"Failed Verticals, Fatal Horizontals, Unreachable Circles of Light: Philip Larkin's Epiphanies." *Moments of Moment: Aspects of the Literary Epiphany*. Edited by Wim Tigges. Amsterdam and Atlanta: DQR Studies in Literature 25, Rodopi P, 1999, 353–374.

"Virtuoso Translations as Visions of Water and Fire: The Elemental Sublime in Swinburne's Arthurian Tale and Bal'mont's Medieval Georgian Epic." *Modern Language Quarterly* 59 (1998): 419–443.

Patterns of Epiphany: From Wordsworth to Tolstoy, Pater, and Barrett Browning. Carbondale: Southern Illinois UP, 1997. Contains essays on Wordsworth, Coleridge, Arnold, Tennyson, Pater, Carlyle, Tolstoy, Barrett Browning.

"Fire and Water, Aspiration and Oblivion: Bal'mont's Re-envisioning of Edgar Allan Poe." *Slavic and East European Journal* 35 (Summer 1991): 193–213.

"Lucy in a Cave on Snowdon: Wordsworth's Inclusive Märchen-Epiphany." *The Wordsworth Circle* 19 (Summer 1988): 111–115.

"Radiant Geometry in Wordsworthian Epiphanies." *The Wordsworth Circle* 16 (Summer 1985): 114–120.

"Parrots, Pictures, Rays, Perfumes: Epiphanies in George Sand and Flaubert." *Studies in Short Fiction* 22 (Spring 1985): 209–217.

"Diminishing Epiphanies of Odin: Carlyle's Reveries of Primal Fire." *Modern Language Quarterly* 44 (Spring 1983): 51–64.

"The Structure of Epiphanic Imagery in Ten Coleridge Lyrics." *Studies in Romanticism* 22 (Spring 1983): 29–40.

"The Central Fiery Heart: Ruskin's Remaking of Dante." *The Victorian Newsletter* No. 48 (Fall 1975): 9–15.

Made in United States
Orlando, FL
13 March 2024